2 3 4 5 **6** 7 8 9 10

HE TECH SET

ryssa Kroski, Series Editor

#6

Technology Training in Libraries

CO-ARS-202

Sarah Houghton-Jan

lita

Neal-Schuman Publishers, Inc.

New York   London

Published by Neal-Schuman Publishers, Inc.
100 William St., Suite 2004
New York, NY 10038

Published in cooperation with the Library Information and Technology Association, a division of the American Library Association.

Printed and bound in the United States of America.

The paper used in this publication meets the minimum requirements of American National Standard for Information Sciences—Permanence of Paper for Printed Library Materials, ANSI Z39.48-1992.

ISBN: 978-1-55570-706-4

For e., whose love makes everything possible

CONTENTS

Don't miss this book's companion wiki and podcast!

Turn the page for details.

THE TECH SET is more than the book you're holding!

All 10 titles in THE TECH SET series feature three components:

1. the book you're now holding;
2. companion wikis to provide even more details on the topic and keep our coverage of this topic up-to-date; and
3. author podcasts that will extend your knowledge and let you get to know the author even better.

The companion wikis and podcasts can be found at:

techset.wetpaint.com

At **techset.wetpaint.com** you'll be able to go far beyond the printed pages you're now holding and:

- ▶ access regular updates from each author that are packed with new advice and recommended resources;
- ▶ use the wiki's forum to interact, ask questions, and share advice with the authors and your LIS peers; and
- ▶ hear these gurus' own words when you listen to THE TECH SET podcasts.

To receive regular updates about TECH SET technologies and authors, sign up for THE TECH SET Facebook page (**facebook.com/ nealschumanpub**) and Twitter (**twitter.com/nealschumanpub**).

For more information on THE TECH SET series and the individual titles, visit **www.neal-schuman.com/techset**.

FOREWORD

Welcome to volume 6 of The Tech Set.

Emerging technologies enable libraries to create innovative new services which leverage the technology that patrons are currently using. But in order for libraries to remain relevant in this information age, librarians must be knowledgeable about these cutting-edge tools and trends. *Technology Training in Libraries* is an essential resource that outlines the steps to creating effective training programs from simple lunchtime brown bags to formal 23 Things courses, technology petting zoos, and peer trainer programs. Tech trainer extraordinaire Sarah Houghton-Jan guides readers through the complete process from how to pace courses, address different learning styles, and deal with difficult learners to ways to communicate expectations from library management. The author is mindful of limited library budgets and provides the most cost-effective strategies for achieving a culture of learning at your library.

The idea for The Tech Set book series developed because I perceived a need for a set of practical guidebooks for using today's cutting-edge technologies specifically within libraries. When I give talks and teach courses, what I hear most from librarians who are interested in implementing these new tools in their organizations are questions on how exactly to go about doing it. A lot has been written about the benefits of these new 2.0 social media tools, and at this point librarians are intrigued but they oftentimes don't know where to start.

I envisioned a series of books that would offer accessible, practical information and would encapsulate the spirit of a 23 Things program but go a step further—to teach librarians not only how to use these programs as individual users but also how to plan and implement particular types of library services using them. I thought it was important to discuss the entire life cycle of these initiatives, including everything from what it takes to plan, strategize, and gain buy-in, to how to develop and implement, to how to market and measure the success of these projects. I also wanted them to incorporate a broad range of project ideas and instructions.

Each of the ten books in The Tech Set series was written with this format in mind. Throughout the series, the "Implementation" chapters, chock-full of detailed project instructions, will be of major interest to all readers. These chapters start off with a basic "recipe" for how to effectively use the technology in a library, and then build on that foundation to offer more and more advanced project ideas. I believe that readers of all levels of expertise will find something useful here as the proposed projects and initiatives run the gamut from the basic to the cutting-edge.

I have been reading and learning from Sarah's insightful LibrarianinBlack blog for years and have been inspired by her presentations at numerous library events. And I cheered along with everyone else in the field when she was named a 2009 Library Journal Mover and Shaker. When I identified that the series needed a book on how to train staff on all of these new and innovative technologies, I knew right away that Sarah was the person to write it. She has been an authority on staff tech training in the library field for many years and this is evident in her exceptional book *Technology Training in Libraries*. Sarah went above and beyond the parameters that I outlined for this title and produced *the* go-to resource for developing tech training programs in libraries.

Ellyssa Kroski
Information Services Technologist
Barnard College Library
www.ellyssakroski.com
http://oedb.org/blogs/ilibrarian
ellyssakroski@yahoo.com

Ellyssa Kroski is an Information Services Technologist at Barnard College as well as a writer, educator, and international conference speaker. She is an adjunct faculty member at Long Island University, Pratt Institute, and San Jose State University where she teaches LIS students about emerging technologies. Her book *Web 2.0 for Librarians and Information Professionals* was published in February 2008, and she is the creator and Series Editor for The Tech Set 10-volume book series. She blogs at iLibrarian and writes a column called "Stacking the Tech" for *Library Journal*'s Academic Newswire.

▶

PREFACE

Libraries have become the technology epicenter of many communities—providing both free access to technology such as the Web and free access to technology training workshops and skill-building resources. Libraries are often the only bridge spanning the digital divide.

Yet, community members often know more about the technology used in libraries than library staff do. Technology training is an important issue that many library administrators face, yet fail to adequately address.

As a technology trainer, I often hear stories of what can happen when a library staff is poorly trained. With the ever-increasing presence of Web 2.0, I believe it is necessary that all libraries implement a comprehensive technology training program. Unfortunately, with budgets being cut and with many in the library world fearful of the unforeseen staffing and funding demands, providing adequate and ongoing technology training for library staff may seem an impossibility.

▶ ORGANIZATION AND AUDIENCE

I wrote *Technology Training in Libraries* to supply librarians with the tools they need to provide the most effective and dollar-conscious technology training for their colleagues. The pages that follow feature answers to commonly asked technology training questions, pertinent information about the latest library technologies, and inspiring case studies that show how providing staff training facilitates the best possible technology-centered customer service.

While the responsibility for "keeping up" with technology has traditionally been placed on the individual library employee, libraries— if they want to remain relevant—should assume responsibility for training staff in technology. For example, if the library introduces a new technology to staff or to the public, the library has the responsibility to create a technology training atmosphere that gives library employees the time and resources they need to learn about it, play with it, poke it, punch it, or even break it if necessary.

Chapter 1 covers the various types of technology training in libraries, including determining what training is needed. Chapter 2 details the approaches for creating a technology skills list for different library positions and how to use those lists to create successful technology training programs. Chapter 3 provides straightforward how-to approaches to integrate several types of popular technology training programs: basic training, lunchtime brown bags, peer training, train-the-trainer programs, the "23 Things" model, technology petting zoos, and the utilization of online training sources.

Chapter 4 covers the best ways to market a technology training program to supporters and skeptics, alike. Chapter 5 covers technology training best practices: whether working with different learning styles, dealing with difficult learners, or conquering training location issues. Chapter 6 defines ways to measure the success of a technology training program, and provided at the end is a list of recommended resources on various features of technology training, which provides excellent supplemental materials.

This book is designed as a one-stop source for technology trainers, human resource coordinators, library managers, and technology-minded staff. It is hoped you will find the information in this book invaluable when providing technology training services for other non-technology-minded employees. Fostering a thriving learning culture is fulfilling for the trainer and will greatly further the library's mission and services.

▶1

INTRODUCTION: TECHNOLOGY TRAINING BASICS

▶ The Benefits of Technology Training

▶ Technology Training Your Library Needs

▶ Typical Technology Topics

▶ Areas of Future Growth

▶ Unscheduled versus Scheduled Training

▶ Technology's Role in Your Library

▶THE BENEFITS OF TECHNOLOGY TRAINING

The question I am asked the most by library managers when I speak about technology training is "Why should I invest staff time and budget money on technology training?" Oppositely, the question I am asked most by library staff is "Why won't our managers provide the technology training we need?" Irrespective of the answers, the bottom line is that the library should provide the best possible customer service to its patrons. Library users have been eagerly waiting for libraries to provide excellent technology services. A well-trained staff can save the library money by performing services at a higher level of proficiency. All managers like to save money and time, but giving the staff the knowledge to provide the best customer assistance is what is most important.

But wait, there's more! Management owes it to all of its employees to clearly define what is expected of them with regard to technology. Technology is always changing and is therefore one of those more difficult "skill groups" to define and train. However, when all library staff understand what managers expect from them, they are likely to perform at a level consistent with those expectations. By offering consistent opportunities for technology training, employees feel that they are a part of a culture of learning in the workplace. Many in the field have spoken or written about the need for libraries to commit to lifelong learning for all staff. But how many have followed through? Ongoing learning must be a priority for each of us, both personally and professionally. However, creating an institutional culture where learning and applying new skills are encouraged can help libraries to obtain, and retain, the staff that will thrive. As Bruce Massis said, "If you're not helping them learn, you're helping them leave" (Massis, 2001: 49). If the staff is more knowledgeable, the level of customer service patrons receive will be consistently excellent.

For those of us with managers who like to see numbers—and let's face it, we all do—there are some established ways to roughly measure the return on investment (ROI) for training dollars spent. The good news is that nearly every study ever done on staff training shows that the ROI is positive. To measure the ROI for your library's existing or proposed training programs, use the following simplified approach. The ROI for any type of training is the same: *Training ROI = the Customer's Value Perception ÷ Cost of Investment*. There is no real right way to calculate ROI, but try to follow these five steps to keep it simple:

1. Calculate the dollar cost of training.
2. Decide what benefits you wish to measure.
3. Record statistics for the benefits before and after training (this is crucial).
4. Calculate the dollar value of the benefits.
5. Determine the cost/benefit ratio.

The Cost of Investment can be determined quite easily. Count these factors when determining the cost of technology training:

▶ Trainer/consultant salaries or payments
▶ Trainee salaries for time in training and travel costs/time

▶ Course administrative costs (scheduling replacement staff, registration)

▶ Course marketing costs (marketing time and materials—flyers, e-mails, etc.)

▶ Course development costs in time and materials

▶ Training materials (handouts, copying, office supplies for trainees)

▶ Facilities costs (rentals, power, lights, etc.)

▶ Equipment costs (e.g., A/V equipment, software, servers/hosting)

For example, let us consider a one-hour online class on Microsoft Word for ten employees, all library assistants. The training cost comes to $1,980.00 for salaries (for the ten staff while they are away from their regular duties) and $20.00 for administration (time spent on registration and scheduling replacement staff). Total = $2,000.00.

The Customer's Value Perception is infinitely more difficult to determine. Measuring the impact on library customers is not as simple as measuring increased sales numbers or profits. The following categories can be used to measure the Customer's Value Perception, but the dollar values assigned to each will necessarily be more subjective as there are few hard and fast numbers to measure something like customer satisfaction:

▶ **Staff productivity**: Time required to complete various tasks, quality and impact of output (also consider the shelf life of the skill and how often it is completed)

▶ **Staff self-sufficiency**: Ability to complete tasks without additional on-the-spot assistance from other staff members

▶ **Staff satisfaction**: Improved job satisfaction, better communication, organizational commitment, and teamwork

▶ **Customer productivity**: Time required to complete various tasks, quality and impact of output

▶ **Customer self-sufficiency**: Ability to complete tasks without assistance from staff

▶ **Customer satisfaction**: Experiential satisfaction ratings from surveys or sampling

> ▶ **Market share**: Customer use of library resources (e.g., card registrations, Web site use, software use, holds placed, etc.)

> ▶ **Downtime**: Hours of equipment downtime due to fixable failures

> ▶ **Employee retention**: Difference in turnover rates attributable to training opportunities

Returning to our example of an online Word class, let's use some conservative figures for our benefits. Staff productivity for our ten trainees has an increased value of $1,000.00 for faster task completion over the next year. Staff self-sufficiency has an increased value of $500.00. Customer productivity (as our staff in turn train customers) has a value of $3,000.00. Customer self-sufficiency has an increased value of $1,500.00. Downtime for this software is reduced for a value of $2,000.00. Total = $8,000.00.

The ROI for this class for the following year is a very realistic 4:1 ($8,000.00 benefit ÷ $2,000.00 cost). For every $1.00 spent on this training, we have gained $4.00 in increased output through our staff and customers.

When reviewing potential costs and benefits to measure, be sure to limit the number of data points to stay as realistic and simple as possible. In addition, use your library's organizational goals and mission statements to guide what those measurable benefits will be. Finally, stick to conservative numbers instead of inflating statistics into surrealistic exercises in futility that no one believes. There are, of course, many more training costs or benefits that may work for your library. This list should at least provide a starting point for determining a quantifiable benefit of providing technology training to your staff.

Another reason to provide technology training to your staff is to relieve what I call your "tech pack mules." These are the staff (in positions of all kinds) who have kept pace with technological changes in the workplace and as a result end up as the go-to-folks for any and all technology questions and tasks. These employees are not compensated for their extra work; they don't get a reduction in their regular work duties for picking up the techie work of others. And yet, these are the very staff that the library so desperately needs to keep in order to provide good customer service. By offering technology training, the library shows the "tech pack mules" that technology training is important to the library, and the rest of the staff are trained up to par so that they can handle more and more situations on their own.

Most of all, having staff members who are not adequately trained in technology trying to support library users is like having a cardboard egg carton holding up an SUV. Our library services are so interwoven with technology that a lack of skill in this area equates to a systematic weakness that can bring the whole structure crashing to the ground. Let's build up that structure, that support, and those skills.

▶ TECHNOLOGY TRAINING YOUR LIBRARY NEEDS

Many people complain about training at their libraries, especially if it is mandatory and they don't feel that it is applicable to their jobs. As a result, I want to talk a bit about the concept of use-based technology training. Use-based training is a system in which you ask the employees what they feel they need to be trained in and consult with their supervisors to finalize that list. The supervisor consultation is meant to ensure that opportunities are not being missed simply because the employee does not know what she needs to know. The resulting feedback from each employee can be used to create a training program that addresses the needs of the staff as a whole through group training, and individual needs can be handled with peer-training or one-on-one sessions that address particular missing technology skills. A similar approach could be used with library customers—survey customers to find out what kind of technology skills training they need in their lives and then focus on offering that type of training. Focusing on what the staff member *wants* to learn, and on what the staff member *needs to know*, is important for the retention rate of the information presented during the training. In short, if people care about what they are being taught, they will be interested, learn more, and retain it for a longer period of time.

▶ TYPICAL TECHNOLOGY TOPICS

Technology training can cover everything from telephones to printer troubleshooting to programming languages. However, a number of key topics are ever-present in good library technology training programs. These topics tend to be those that are most essential to library operations and successful staff performance. Following is a list of essential and "Wow—I'd really like to offer . . ." technology training topics. Note that by placing topics in the second category I am not saying that they are not important to library customer service. On the contrary, they are increasingly important. However, in an environment where resources are limited, a tiered approach and identification of topics that are *truly essential to basic library operations* was formulated. Any library of any type or size can take this list as a starting point, build on it to meet your library's unique needs, and then start finding, creating, and offering training to your staff. You can approach public technology training in a similar fashion—focus on a "must have" list of topics first, and then move on to the desired but less requested topics. Instant public training program plan!

Essential Technology Training Topics in Libraries

- Technology terminology
- Operating systems used on staff and public-use computers
- Library's integrated library system (circulation, WebPac, plus specialized topics)
- E-mail system used by staff, as well as common Web-based e-mail providers
- Web browsers on staff and public-use computers
- Search skills applicable in Web browsers, WebPac, databases, and other systems
- Office-type software (word processing, spreadsheet, and presentation software)
- Hardware, including computers, peripherals, printers, photocopiers, fax machines, and phones
- Troubleshooting of software and hardware in use in the library
- File management skills for operating system and e-mail system

- ▶ Security issues, including systems on staff and public-use computers as well as potential security and privacy threats present via computer and Internet use
- ▶ Library's e-resources for the public and staff (e.g., eBooks, databases, intranet)
- ▶ Library's technology-related policies and procedures
- ▶ Ergonomics

"Wow—I'd Really Like to Offer . . ." Technology Training Topics

- ▶ Social networking and "the social Web"
- ▶ Blogging and microblogging
- ▶ Instant messaging services
- ▶ Text messaging services
- ▶ Networking architecture, optimization, and other issues
- ▶ RSS
- ▶ Next-generation library WebPac opportunities
- ▶ Tagging/folksonomies
- ▶ The semantic Web
- ▶ Legal, ethical, and social issues such as copyright, licensing, Net neutrality, open access, and open source
- ▶ Dealing with change and continuous learning
- ▶ Online outreach and marketing
- ▶ User technology training tips
- ▶ Mobile devices

▶ AREAS OF FUTURE GROWTH

As technology changes and evolves, so should technology training. Some of the emerging topics that libraries should keep on their radar for staff training include the following:

- ▶ Cloud computing
- ▶ Surface computing
- ▶ Open source software development

> ▶ APIs (application programming interfaces) and their intersection with library services)
> ▶ RFID (radio frequency identification) technologies
> ▶ New models of user authorization and authentication

Keep an eye out for new topics being mentioned on library blogs and other social media. If you see it mentioned twice, write it down. Three times means it warrants some discussion as a potential training topic for staff.

▶ UNSCHEDULED VERSUS SCHEDULED TRAINING

To me, there are two major types of training: scheduled and unscheduled training. It is difficult, especially for new trainers, to assess which delivery method will be most effective for which topic and audience combination. Scheduled learning works very well for the more basic technology topics, especially those that you feel you can efficiently deliver in groups of 3 to 30. There are various types of scheduled learning that you can utilize with staff, such as:

> ▶ Webcasts
> ▶ Teleconferences
> ▶ Large centralized group training (including hands-on practice, demonstrations, and lectures)
> ▶ Small de-centralized group training (including hands-on practice, demonstrations, and lectures)
> ▶ One-on-one training
> ▶ Daily or weekly "learn by e-mail" tutorials
> ▶ Peer training (sometimes called the train-the-trainer model)
> ▶ Conferences and outside seminars

I often get questions from trainers about whether a particular topic should be taught in person or online, in a small class or a large class. I feel that online can work for just about anything, although, because some learners find it difficult to process information through an online environment, it is best to offer at least a limited number of in-person classes too. The best rule of thumb is to follow your own intuition. How do you learn best? Do you learn better in a large lecture hall or in small group discussions (see Figures 1.1 and 1.2)? Sometimes time and financial constraints may require large lecture formats, but, for the sake of training interactivity and learner retention of the material, I recommend avoiding this style when possible. Ask yourself—how would attendees have a better learning experience?

There are also a number of unscheduled types of training. These tend to get short shrift, as they are seemingly considered less valid by library managers. The result is that library staff are not given time to learn in these ways, staff tend not to schedule themselves to learn this way, and much untapped potential is wasted. Unscheduled learning is the best way to address more advanced topics, especially those where the knowledge level may differ greatly among the various learners. These are the most effective unscheduled learning methods:

▶ Figure 1.1: Large Lecture Hall at the Computers in Libraries Conference, 2008

▶ Figure 1.2: Small Talk Tables for Library Staff Training and Brainstorming, Hawaii Library Association Conference, Kauai, 2007

- ▶ Reading (a book, an article, a listserv, a blog post, etc.)
- ▶ Online tutorials
- ▶ Field trips or virtual communication to see what other nearby libraries are doing
- ▶ Previously recorded Webcasts, podcasts, screencasts, or video-casts
- ▶ Asynchronous online courses

The, what I call, "on-the-spot-oh-gosh-you-gotta-know-this-now" method of learning is not well-retained, usually promotes weak customer service skills, and creates needless stress about technology for the library staff. On-the-spot learning also does not work well for our library patrons. Ideally, we would have more time to work with them and set up more leisurely and structured learning environments where they could maximize technology information retention. However, as in most customer service environments, we play the cards that are dealt. You will likely find yourself endlessly involved in on-the-spot learning with library staff and patrons.

However, the more that we can avoid this learning method with our own staff, and use the others instead, the better we can serve our customers in their moments of need.

▶ TECHNOLOGY'S ROLE IN YOUR LIBRARY

Few would argue against technology's place in libraries. However, technology training has not managed to make its way into very many libraries, especially not in a coordinated manner. The fact that most libraries still have staff today who are not comfortable operating the programs they use every day in their work, including helping users with the library's technology offerings, is not only unacceptable but also points to the library's own failings in training its staff to meet those expectations. We can point the finger at a lack of enough funding, and therefore often a lack of staff time, as the reason that library staff are not adequately trained. However, once again I come back to customer service. With user contacts that involve staff members demonstrating incompetence with the resources the library offers, the library not only looks incompetent, but the library becomes less of a reliable resource for the future. This nightmare is what all libraries strive to avoid.

By offering adequate technology training, staff will obtain adequate technology skills and therefore offer technology-related customer service that the library can be proud of. The bottom line is that the technology services we provide to our users should not be treated as "extra" or second class by any of us. Technology has been around a long time in libraries, and it is here to stay. Let's use this to our advantage and make our communities proud.

▶2

PLANNING

- ▶ Develop a Technology Skills List
- ▶ Prioritize Training
- ▶ Create an Organizational Technology Training Plan
- ▶ Create a Staff Learning and Innovation Plan
- ▶ Provide Effective Technology Training

▶ DEVELOP A TECHNOLOGY SKILLS LIST

A technology skills list is an easy and efficient way to organize an ongoing technology training program at your library. Technology skills, or competencies, are the technology-related abilities, qualities, strengths, and skills required for the success of the employee and the organization. As you might imagine, these skills have increased in number with the advent of personal computers, the Internet, and Web 2.0. Technology skills are crucial for the success of any organization—but critically important for successful customer service in libraries. Building a skills list is part of the "Analyze" stage of the widely accepted and popular training development method called **ADDIE: A**nalyze **D**esign, **D**evelop, **I**mplement, and **E**valuate. Using a skills list has many benefits for the library, employees, and customers.

Benefits of the Skills List Approach

Save the Library Money

I'll start with the most important benefit—money! If the library can train each staff member to handle a simple network outage (rebooting routers, modems, and hubs), then that could save the library some of those pricey $200.00 calls to the network support staff. The library will also save time (and time is money) in the long run through the ability to train many people on topics simultaneously. Instead of 20 individuals getting one-on-one training from a peer in the library "on the spot" (usually not the ideal time or situation for learning a new skill), one trainer can impart the knowledge to 20 individuals in one fell swoop. A good manager is fiscally responsible; training staff on technology is fiscally responsible. Therefore, a good manager trains his or her staff. For more on money, see Chapter 1's coverage of training's return on investment.

Create Clear Expectations from Library Management

A well-defined set of technology skills expectations can help employees understand managers' priorities. When employees understand exactly what it is that managers expect from them, they are much more likely to perform at a level consistent with those expectations. Skills lists can also help managers understand what is expected of the people they supervise, especially in situations where a nontechnical supervisor is supervising technical staff.

Create Accurate Job Descriptions

The utilization of a technology skills list can provide a better way to build accurate job descriptions or classification systems. The skills identified, be they general or specific, can be inherently tied to the job descriptions for the various staff positions—including volunteers. If the library decides to post its technology skills lists online on the open Web, you can also link to these from job ads, thus giving prospective candidates a very clear picture of exactly what you will expect from them in terms of technology skills on the job. By simply adding one line to all of the library's job descriptions, something like, "Meets and practices the library's core staff technology skills," the library can quickly begin to recruit individuals who meet the needs of the organization and its users. Interview panels can also highlight key skills in the interview process and ask questions to gauge the candidate's readiness.

Create a Culture of Learning in Your Library

Technologies are changing quickly, and our staff need to be able to keep up. Unfortunately, we don't live in a world where technologies move from one to another quickly and completely. Much has been written about the need for libraries to show a commitment to lifelong learning for all staff. Library schools are now turning out students who are technologically skilled, and this helps somewhat. But in order to reassert our profession as one of knowledgeable information-finding experts, we need to take full advantage of continuing education for each and every library staff member in every type of library. Ongoing learning must be a priority for each of us, both personally and professionally.

Finding staff who meet these criteria is tough; keeping them is even harder. Creating an institutional culture where learning and experimenting are encouraged is a principle way of doing both. Creating a culture of learning in your own library includes many components. Beyond the basics of a technology skills training program, you must also consider budgeting adequately for training, offering training in-house, promoting external training opportunities, giving staff ample time to attend or complete physical and virtual trainings, supporting professional development that isn't strictly defined as training (conferences, user groups, reading professional literature), and having staff cross-train each other and share the information they've learned, both formally and informally. Creating a technology (or other) skills list and using that as the basis for a coordinated training program will also contribute to that culture. Having concrete and uniform expectations can unify the staff across various units and departments and help to improve the sharing of knowledge and skills among staff members.

Help Out the Tech Pack Mules

The problem of unequal technology workloads occurs when, over time, staff have not all kept pace with the fast current of technological change in the workplace, when new staff are hired who are ill-equipped to deal with the technologies in the workplace, and when library schools turn out students unprepared for the technology demands of the profession. That will always be the case, but holding everyone on staff to a set of technology skills can level the playing field dramatically. This is essential because of the tech pack mules in your organizations. Regardless of their official positions in the organization, they tend to be the person that everyone else on staff calls when something needs fixing or a user needs tech-specific help. These pack mules become tired, angry, and resentful that their workloads are greater than their counterparts' and they are never acknowledged or rewarded for it. These are the types of employees, highly technically proficient, that we desperately need to keep in our libraries. By overloading them with extra tasks and work, however, the library risks losing them.

Improve Customer Service

Many of us in libraries are acting as first line, de facto tech support. If we do not have a handle on the technology tools that we use, the technology gets in the way of our service to our users and things don't run smoothly. We want everyone on our staff to be able to help our users equally. Our technology skills need to be so second nature to us, to each of us, that they come as naturally as breathing. By getting everyone on the same page with their technology skills, the library creates a frontline force with technology know-how, expertise, and ability, each one ready to step in and solve whatever problem or question comes up—*right then and there.* No more shuffling a user from one person to another or making the user wait minutes, even days, for an answer. The library gets out of the unenviable position of relying on one or two tech-savvy staff people to do and know everything technology-oriented.

Build a Coordinated Training Program

Many of us have been doing things piecemeal to learn as we go along. We're slowly trying to learn what we need to know—we're all trying. But some guidance in this area would be most helpful, no? Some idea of what we're actually expected to know would go a long way toward building confidence and allaying fears. Having a set of technology skills gives you something to use to determine current skill sets versus desired skill sets, your status quo versus your status ideal. If your library lacks a coordinated technology training program and is adding new technologies to the workplace (what library isn't?), then having a technology skills list is your ticket to stardom. The library will know which skills to teach, and to whom, and the categories you created for the skills divide nicely into categories for individual training sessions.

Elements of an Effective Skills List

There are many different ways to create, format, and organize your skills lists. Here are some of the key elements you need to think about.

Descriptive versus Task-Based Content

Descriptive skills are broad and nonspecific (e.g., "Understand how e-mail folders work to create an organized file-keeping system"). Task-based skills, on the other hand, are narrowly focused and specific (e.g., "Delete e-mails, move e-mails between folders, and archive old e-mails"). The most successful skills lists will include both task-based items as well as more descriptive overriding philosophical and knowledge skills that contribute to a successful technologically proficient employee.

Verbs

Action verbs are easy to measure. "Can you X? Can you Y?" Use action verbs when you can.

Sentence Structure

Whatever structure the taskforce decides on, use consistent formatting for each skill (e.g., have an action verb as the first word in the sentence/phrase like "Understand, Reboot, Search, Create, Troubleshoot" and also have certain phrases you use consistently like "Demonstrates a knowledge of," "Ability to," and "Familiarity with"). Consistency is key.

Word Choice

Use consistent wording in your skills so that as little is subjective as possible. Be careful of your use of adjectives, which can be interpreted subjectively and differently by each individual. Try to be as objective and quantitative as you can with the skills. Additionally, do not phrase any of the assessments, purpose statements, or questions in the format "Are you competent?" Just as libraries are moving away from the term "information literacy" (as it requires users to admit "illiteracy" in order to use our services), talking about "incompetency" and "competency" can easily put people off of the entire program before they even begin. Instead of calling them "competencies," as was popular in the past, as I indeed did myself for a long time, call them a "technology learning checklist" or a "technology training plan." It all depends on the staff environment of your individual library.

One Level versus Multiple Levels Format

The skills list can have one or multiple levels. Some are simple, direct lists of what staff need to know or be able to do. Another option is to break the skills out into various levels or tiers, and which staff members need to meet which tier may be based on position, desire for promotion, or personal preference. If the library decides to use a multilevel system, the taskforce may want to define who needs to have the more advanced skills based on a few different factors, such as staff classification, specific position, work location, pay step, or desire for promotion/bonus.

Organization by Position, Department, Location

If the skills list has different sections based on staff position, department, or location, then organizing the skills by position may be the easiest way to present that information. Skills may be broken out by staff position (Library Assistant 1, Librarian 2, Branch Manager), by more general department (managers, reference staff [adult, children's, teen], technical services, circulation), or by location (smaller branches vs. main branch). If the library is writing skills lists for a small library, or there are one or more small libraries in the library system, keep in mind that in small libraries where there are only one or two people working at once, staff position doesn't matter nearly as much. Everyone has to be a generalist. Everyone might have to know everything. As Charlene McGuire (2005) writes in a post to the Kansas Tech Consultants Blog, with the first draft of the Technology Core Skills for Kansas Library Workers, "If it is a one person library then that is the person." It's important to make sure that the skills reflect the reality at each library, big or small. You may also want to consider having a basic list of skills by staff position, with supervisory flexibility to add or remove other skills based on that person's unique job situation (e.g., a circulation staff where everyone's tasks are broken out so one person might never deal with the ILS or another may never need to use a word processing program).

With or Without an Assessment Tool

You can choose to present the skills alone or combine the skills with the assessment tool. If the taskforce decides to combine the skills list with the assessment tool, remember to provide space at the top of the list for the employee's name, and perhaps unit/department, start and/or completion dates, or general comments or questions from the employee. You can do this in a table format, an outline, a narrative paragraph, a grid, or a checklist. Use whatever works best for your goals.

How to Create a Skills List

Create a Taskforce

I don't like committees. I don't like taskforces. But, they are a necessary evil sometimes. Some organizations have left the creation of technology skills lists to one person on staff, such as a manager, a technology support person, or a training coordinator. I highly recommend against this one-person approach for two key reasons. First, that person will be overwhelmed with the amount of work required for this process. Second, the quality of the end product increases when you add more brainpower to it. Instead, create a small skills taskforce, composed of representatives from the various departments and/or staff positions within your institution. I think it is essential to tap the knowledge of the staff who work on the front lines and those who are technologically expert. Both of their contributions to the taskforce will be invaluable.

The taskforce should schedule regular face-to-face meetings (biweekly or monthly seems to be the preference for most libraries) but also be available to communicate electronically via e-mail or instant messaging. The taskforce may also wish to consider setting up a wiki, discussion board, or blog to foster communication about the project and to preserve the process as it occurs.

Conduct a Literature Review

Each member of the taskforce should be given some required reading. Now this is very, very important: this reading should be done on *work time*, not personal time. Here are some of the things the taskforce could consider reading:

▶ Review two to five technology skills lists from other libraries.

▶ Review one to three general skills lists from the relevant professional organizations.

▶ Review two to five articles about technology and skills lists.

Write a Purpose Statement to Guide Your Work

Why are you creating a set of technology skills lists? This is the first question that the taskforce needs to answer. The taskforce's first meeting should consist of brainstorming possible elements of a purpose statement, hopefully ending the meeting with one in hand. The purpose statement can guide the planning process and serve as a beacon document as the taskforce moves forward. The purpose statement can also match up with the library's strategic goals and objectives. The purpose statement should be disseminated to all staff—along with a brief explanation of the process and the taskforce's activities.

Here are some possible elements to include in a purpose statement:

▶ All the benefits to this approach that we discussed earlier

▶ Helping staff meet user needs

▶ Stimulating service excellence

▶ Answering the question, "What do I need to know to do my job?"

▶ Explaining the components for success in a job

▶ Planning continuous staff development

▶ Improving the staff's ability to be self-sufficient

▶ Educating others (e.g., governing bodies and users) about what we do

Set a Timeline

Once a purpose statement has been created, the taskforce should create a realistic timeline. The taskforce should set a date by which it wishes to accomplish each of the steps the group plans to complete. I suggest that the overall process, from writing the purpose statement to developing a training plan based on the self-assessments, should take no longer than six months. Depending on the size of your library, you may be able to complete this in much less time, and, if that's the case, more power to you.

Assess Local Requirements

Find out from administration which governing and other deci-sion-making bodies may need to approve the skills lists before they are implemented. Groups may include your commission or board, a parent organization like a county or city board of supervisors or a university regulations board, the library's administrative team, spe-cific staff members (like the director), and your employee unions. Many libraries now have unionized employees, perhaps even em-ployees in more than one union. Determine early in the process if the union needs to formally approve anything you put in place or if perhaps approval is only required if the skills lists are tied to pay increases and decreases or promotions/demotions. This is an *extremely* important step in the process—and not one to be missed or taken lightly.

Hold a Staff Brainstorming Session

What do staff think is important within the library to know? People love to talk. So . . . let them. Staff know best what they need to know to do their jobs. Surprisingly (or perhaps not) they don't all agree on what they need to know for a particular position, but the person doing the job day to day has the most information about what skills are required to do that job successfully. Set up a three-hour (or more if you can!) brainstorming session at a central location, one that is convenient for as many staff members as possible. Several independent brainstorming sessions are likely to bring about very different lists as well, so you may want to consider holding regional or departmental brainstorming sessions. Try holding several open brainstorming sessions either in person or online through a wiki, blog, or discussion board (communicating in person allows for a live-interaction dynamic you often don't find online).

Invite everyone to participate—*everyone*. If every staff position is going to be beholden to the skills lists, you want people from every position to be there. Have large markers and large pieces of butcher paper available (those lovely tear-off sheets that fit on ea-sels are perfect), and write everything that is said on these pieces of paper. Most importantly—have plenty of refreshments! Seat participants in a circle if at all possible (this will lend to the atmo-sphere of equality and sharing). Start the session off by reiterating the purpose statement, letting staff know of the decisions the taskforce has made regarding scope of the skills and that this is a brainstorming session and should be treated as such. This means that any idea goes, judgments and arguments should *not* be made at this point about specific ideas, and all contributions are equally valued. Anything goes. Ask staff what they are looking for in technology training. What topics do staff want training on? What do staff think is important within the library to know? What training methods do they feel work best for them? After the session, have one of the taskforce members transcribe everything into a word processing document or a spreadsheet, whatever seems to make more sense given the data you've gathered. The taskforce should discuss these results at a future meeting and take them heavily into consideration during the creation process.

Survey Staff

After the brainstorming sessions, the taskforce may find that it needs more information from staff. If you find yourself in this position, or if you are unable to conduct an in-person brainstorming session, consider creating an anonymous survey for staff. Using free online survey tools like SurveyMonkey and Zoomerang can allow the taskforce to quickly gather and analyze data on remaining questions.

I recommend that the survey be structured in one of two ways. (1) Ask staff if they would attend trainings on specific topics, for example, "Would you participate in a training about using Flickr in the library, which might include editing and uploading photos, organizing photos using collections and sets, and using Flickr as a marketing tool?" (2) Ask staff in a free-response question to state what topics they feel they need training on. Each option results in different data.

In addition to their free, basic accounts, SurveyMonkey (www.surveymonkey.com) and Zoomerang (www.zoomerang.com) both offer a number of more sophisticated options for a price. Larger libraries will likely need one of these.

Depending on the atmosphere of your library, and the goals for the survey, it might be most effective if the responses are anonymous. However, having individual-specific data can more effectively help managers evaluate and create training goals for employees. The taskforce might want to target questions at specific positions. For example, ask only circulation workers whether or not they feel they all, at all levels, need to know how to troubleshoot printing from a Web page. The taskforce will know what it needs to ask once the members have gone over the results of the brainstorming. This staff survey may come before or after the taskforce has created a draft technology skills list, so this step may come slightly out of order.

Create a Technology Needs Pyramid

Aaron Schmidt conceived of the idea of creating a Technology Needs Pyramid to outline the library's technology needs and goals (Schmidt, 2005). Just like the Maslow Hierarchy of Needs, Technology Needs Pyramids outline the most critical needs at the base level, with additional layers building the rest of the pyramid in decreasing orders of necessity, culminating in long-term goals or pie-in-the sky desires for library technology. Figure 2.1 shows an example of a simplified pyramid for a library Web site. Working with such a document can be extremely helpful in creating and visualizing the library's technology plan but can serve a dual purpose as a method to determine what technologies the library staff

▶ Figure 2.1: Simplified Technology Needs Pyramid Showing Library Web Services

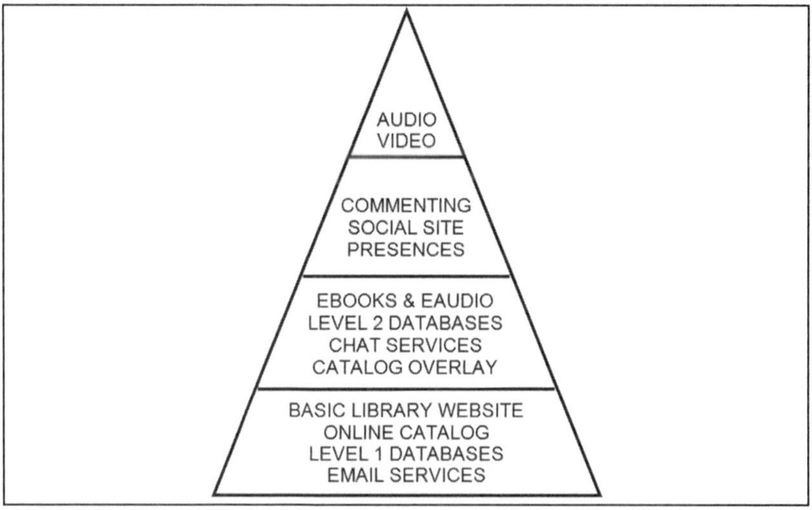

AUDIO
VIDEO

COMMENTING
SOCIAL SITE
PRESENCES

EBOOKS & EAUDIO
LEVEL 2 DATABASES
CHAT SERVICES
CATALOG OVERLAY

BASIC LIBRARY WEBSITE
ONLINE CATALOG
LEVEL 1 DATABASES
EMAIL SERVICES

need training on in order to meet the library's overall technology goals.

How to Write a Skills List

This is the hard part, so strap on your hard hats. The taskforce will draft a rough list of technology skills during this stage of the process. This list will most likely be quite rough, and that's perfectly fine. What we're looking for here is a starting point, a foundation—not perfection.

Create Rough Categories

In looking at the skills listed by the staff, and at some of the categories in other libraries' lists, what categories are emerging as those the library will want to include in its own list? Don't worry at this point about qualitatively analyzing everything that has been suggested. List everything that has been gathered into one list, and break it down into categories. But which categories should you use?

Think about categorizing the skills into these possible rough categories: personal vs. professional, by various service areas, by device or software in question, or by system goals. As an example of how to categorize things, here are the categories in the California Library Association's Technology Skills:

- ▶ Terminology
- ▶ Hardware (parts of the computer, printers, photocopiers, telephones, fax machines)
- ▶ Software (word processing, spreadsheets, multimedia, Web browsers, e-mail, operating system, files and folders)
- ▶ Security
- ▶ Troubleshooting
- ▶ Library resources
- ▶ Search skills
- ▶ Public computers

Once you've created some categories, start plugging in the skills that you have gathered from all your various sources up to this point. New category needs will emerge as you find gaps, and other categories may combine as similarities are found. Remember—everything is flexible. The taskforce is still merely trying to build a draft at this point.

Include Important "Easy to Miss" Areas

Instead of attempting to provide you with an exhaustive list of all the possible technology skills to include, what follows is a list of "must-have" areas that I came across in my research that I feel every organization should have, or at least strongly consider having, in their list.

▶ **Technology terms glossary**: Including a glossary with the technology terminology used not only in the skills themselves, but also on the job day to day, will greatly improve staff's ability to communicate effectively with technical support staff, the public, and each other.

▶ **Dealing with change**: This is a challenge for all of us, but the ability to cope with an ever-changing technological landscape is a skill that is requisite of, in my opinion, each and every staff position in any library.

▶ **Planning and evaluating**: Include skills that address the need for staff to evaluate and plan for new information technology systems. This can range from line staff being able to evaluate two competing databases on a particular subject, to all staff being able to evaluate a new ILS, to management being able to project and plan for the implementation of a new public computer management system.

▶ **Helping remote users**: Include skills that are necessary for helping serve the library's remote users—the users who access the library's resources from home and rarely, if ever, step foot in the physical library building (incidentally, this is the fastest-growing population for every library). This may include techniques and skills necessary to help people with the library's Web-accessible resources, search strategies, and technical troubleshooting remotely.

▶ **Specific software and hardware**: It's easy to think about desktop computers and the software we deal with on a regular basis (word processing, e-mail, and Web browsers) and forget about all the other technology we deal with every day. Don't forget to think about the skills required to use the various software and hardware systems in the library: the various incarnations of the library's ILS, computer reservation software, print management software, self-check-in and self-check-out machines, projectors, cameras, audio and video recorders, RFID, sorting systems, wireless equipment, blogs, wikis, and so on.

▶ **Online reference**: If the library offers virtual reference services, make sure that the skills necessary for these services are listed separately for the staff who provide these services.

▶ **Public and staff views**: Include specifics about technologies that staff need to know how to use from both the staff and public sides, such as the ability to effectively search both the public-facing OPAC as well as the staff interface.

▶ **Policies and law**: Include skills that address local policies and administrative documents as they relate to technology, communication use, the public, and staff behavior/abilities. Also include skills that address local, state, and national laws as they relate to technology, like CIPA (the Children's Internet Protection Act), RFID laws, and copyright laws.

▶ **Ergonomics**: Include skills that address the ergonomic needs of your institution's staff, such as proper chair fitting, desk height, how to avoid repetitive stress injuries, and correct lighting for using computer screens.

▶ **Continuous learning and "keeping up"**: Include a skill that addresses the need for staff to look for opportunities to learn, whether formal or informal, in an effort to keep up-to-date with the needs of the job.

Finalize the Skills

At this point the taskforce needs to go through the list of potential skills and narrow it down, finalizing categories and skills within the categories. Which staff are beholden to which skills should be clearly indicated. If the taskforce has difficulty coming to consensus on particular skills, kick it up the decision-making tree to whatever administrative group or committee exists to make final decisions in cases like these. The taskforce will have to agree to abide by whatever that group decides, however. Sometimes, remembering this is enough to jumpstart the consensus process.

Once the taskforce is confident that the skills are complete, polished, and ready to go, the next step is implementation.

How to Implement a Skills List

Get the Skills Approved

The skills should be sent to each relevant administrative or involved group with a brief letter of introduction, including the purpose statement, the process so far, as well as the taskforce's plans for implementation, including assessment, organizational and individual training plans, and the training itself. Various groups may suggest changes to the skills. After all the hard work the taskforce has put in, it may be difficult to hear newcomers to the project suggesting revisions. These newcomers have a unique view of the library and the staff, and for this reason may see things that the taskforce did not. In some cases, the taskforce may even be required to adopt the changes a group or individual recommends. Keep an open mind and remember—the skills will not be ruined because of one addition or subtraction. The overall project is what the taskforce is concerned with, and at this point, what you have created is a highly valuable tool for the library. That's what matters!

Decide on Incentives and Negative Consequences

This topic is addressed in Chapter 3, but it is important (*before* implementation) to decide on these two issues. Here's a clandestine hint: lean toward incentives.

Present the Skills to Staff

You may be presenting the skills and the assessment at the same time, if you have elected for a combination format, or you may be presenting the skills by themselves first. In either case, this is a crucial step. If you do not achieve staff buy-in at all levels at this point, the creation of the skills list may have little impact on the workplace. The taskforce may want to consider having a kick-off party for the list, including food, music, and a hands-on technology petting zoo where staff can touch all of the technologies they are being expected to use and understand. A more simple approach to presenting the skills is to write a letter similar to the one the taskforce wrote for the groups needing to approve the skills, reiterating the purpose of the skills and explaining what is going to happen next. This letter, along with the skills list, can be distributed to staff members through e-mail, a staff newsletter, staff blog, or even hard copy.

Reassure staff not to worry if there are skills in their area that they don't have, letting them know that training is on its way. Emphasize that the skills are a goal right now, not where all staff are expected to be at this moment. Deliver the new skills in a positive way—stressing how learning these new skills will help the employees themselves, making their work lives easier. You may even want to create a Web page with all the information about the skills: the various skills lists and/or assessment tools, the mission statement, links to training materials, and lists of upcoming trainings.

Finally, getting manager buy-in at every level at this stage is essential. Every staff member who supervises the work of any other staff member needs to believe in the skills and be willing to implement and enforce them. Without uniform application and encouragement in all units and departments, the skills will create only a patchwork of tech-savvy staff members. Others, largely those whose managers do not believe in the project and therefore do not support it, will fall by the wayside and be left behind. No one wants that.

How to Choose a Staff Skills Assessment Method

First, ask if the goal of your institution is to hold specific employees to specific skills to ensure that quality is met on an individual basis *or* if the library wants to gauge only the general training needs of its staff and offer training accordingly. If the library is less concerned about individual accountability, consider taking the shortest route and sending out anonymous questionnaires/assessments to staff in order to determine where the training gaps are in general. If the library is, however, concerned about individual skill levels and accountability, there are several methods for individual assessments available.

Test Staff's Current Skills

Ask questions about knowledge that assesses abilities. Word the assessment questions as objectively as possible. Leave few (preferably no) questions open-ended, where the response could be subjectively evaluated. This means making the questions largely multiple choice, true/false, and labeling (for parts of the computer or screen).

The test can take the form of a simple paper-and-pencil exam. It can also be an online exam created with a free survey/test tool like SurveyMonkey or with software that will actually ask the user to perform certain tasks and track mouse clicks and keyboard strokes to determine if the task was completed correctly.

As much as we would like to believe the best of our coworkers, you will absolutely need to address the possibility of cheating. Users might do a quick Web search to find an answer they don't know or ask a coworker who already took the assessment. If you are truly going to get an objective measurement of an employee's skills, doing so in a controlled test environment is the only way to be 100 percent accurate. The taskforce should consider the opportunities for cheating and eliminate as many of them as possible.

Testing has another serious downside, which is why you see it in very few libraries. Staff members may worry that their score will go on their record, be in their evaluations, or be used against them to unfairly compare them to other staff or to justify their firing. As such, their reaction to the competency process as a whole (trainings included) is much more likely to be hostile, defensive, and generally disgruntled. There are other assessment methods that you can use to avoid this "test and bristle" response.

Assess Current Practice

An excellent method to discover staff technology skills is to ask them about what they do and how often they do it, instead of directly asking if they do or do not have a particular skill. This is particularly helpful if the work environment is one that is felt by the staff to be punitive or when staff feel particularly uncomfortable admitting a lack of knowledge. As an example, surveys could ask users to respond on a scale ranging from "Never" to "Always" to questions such as, "Do you check the staff announcements Web page every day?" or "Do you sort your files into folders within My Documents?" In this way, staff are not only more likely to respond honestly, but the data gathered will be on a sliding scale and therefore easily evaluated. D. Scott Brandt suggests this method and offers additional examples in his book *Teaching Technology: A How-To-Do-It Manual for Librarians* (Brandt, 2002: 14).

Ask Staff to Self-Assess

Most libraries opt for self-assessment for their staff—trusting staff to be honest about what they do and do not know, especially if they have been reassured that "not knowing" at the outset of the implementation of the skills is completely acceptable. However, even in this case, you will still need to watch for staff who misrepresent their knowledge. If the training coordinator or the manager can communicate with people who work with the person on a regular basis, misrepresentation will become clear enough.

When using self-assessments, I recommend avoiding the "Yes I meet it/No I don't meet it" binary that has the potential for garnering inaccurate responses. Here are some alternatives:

- ▶ Have three choices for whether or not the employee meets each competency: Yes, No, or Maybe/Don't know.
- ▶ Ask about the employee's experience with a particular competency, and quantify that with a few choices: None, Little, Some, and A Lot.
- ▶ Ask if employees feel that they meet the various skills in a basic, intermediate, or advanced level.

You are far more likely to get honest responses to these sliding scales than to a pure Yes/No question. If an employee doesn't know something, he or she is more likely to mark "Maybe" than "No." When it comes down to evaluating the assessment results, perhaps a "Maybe" counts the same as a "No," and a "Little" may count just like a "None." The trick is that staff don't necessarily need to know this.

Have Staff Assess Each Other

Another option is to have a supervisor work with the employee and perform what is called an observation assessment. In this model, the supervisor works with the employee on the list of skills, asking the employee to perform or discuss each one, and then the supervisor makes the ultimate judgment as to whether the technology skill has been met or not. One other peer assessment model is to have every employee's skill level evaluated by everyone who works with that person.

Choose an Assessment Format

A decision also needs to be made about how to conduct the assessment. The basic options are paper or online. Doing assessments online is, by far, the most efficient method, and almost every one of the options discussed, except for the first peer-assessment option, can be done online. This can be done with a simple Web form that outputs into a database or with one of the free or fee-based survey sites (that function just as well as test/assessment sites). There are also a number of fee-based software options that will test an employee's skills by asking him or her to perform certain tasks and software that will help you create tests and assessments in a more structured way than the survey sites do, as well as offering more options for manipulating and evaluating the end data.

Offering the assessment online may not be an option, especially if it is seen as a barrier for the lowest-skilled staff. In this case, paper assessments may be offered. Depending on the assessment style you chose, these may be asking employees to check boxes, circle correct answers, or mark the correct level for their ability on a rating scale. Compiling the results of paper assessments can be quite cumbersome, so, if choosing this option, budget appropriate time for doing it.

Tweak Your Assessment Process

When sending out the assessment, if sending separately from the skills, emphasize once again the skills' purpose statement and reassure staff that they are not expected to meet all of the skills right away. Review some of the tips given earlier in this chapter regarding presentation of the skills to staff and use the same tips during assessment.

All employees subject to the skills should be given the assessment at the same time. Give staff a deadline by which they need to return the assessment and consequences if the deadline is not met (e.g., departments that meet the deadline get a pizza party; those that do not sadly get no pizza). I made the mistake of leaving it open-ended the first time I sent out an assessment, and two years later I had still not received an entire unit's assessments, despite consistent badgering. Deadlines make people work faster. It's a law of nature somehow.

All new employees should complete the assessment immediately. This can be added to any "new-hire checklists" that the library may have on file. New-hire assessment results should be discussed with the employee and his or her supervisor, and a training plan developed as a result.

In addition to asking where employees are currently with their skills, consider including additional questions about where they would *like* to be in terms of their technical skills. Be sure to include an open-ended question asking staff what they want to learn that was not listed on the assessment. It may be something super-advanced, something so specialized that it didn't make it onto the assessment, or even something so hipster and new that the library didn't even consider training for it yet. Finally, have one or more questions at the end of the assessment asking staff if there are particular areas that they feel like they would actually like more training on or in which they would like to see self-improvement—including areas not described in the skills. What do staff *want* to learn? This is important information for any trainer.

Share the Assessment Results

If assessments were not self-assessments, employees should most definitely see the results of their assessments. Each unit manager and immediate supervisor should be given the assessment results of the employees they supervise. Results should also, of course, be given to the training coordinator or the equivalent manager of the skills project. A secure password-protected file should be kept that records the exact results for each staff member. If the assessments were made with an appropriate online tool, you may be lucky enough to have a nice spreadsheet ready-made with everyone's results. These initial assessments should be kept as a baseline to which to compare future assessments.

The training coordinator also needs to look at the overall patterns in the assessment results. These overall patterns should also be kept as a baseline to which to compare future assessments. But more than that, the overall patterns should be examined to identify training needs. How many staff members need training on which topics? Which trainings can be provided in-house? Of these, how much staff time is going to be required to prepare the necessary materials for the classes? Which trainings will require bringing in outside trainers or sending staff to off-site training? These and other questions will need to be answered as we move into the training phase of the skills process. The training coordinator, the skills taskforce, and the library's management will need to realistically discuss the emergent training needs of the library staff and what it will take to meet those needs. We're talking staffing and budget recommendations at this point.

Update Skills Lists Regularly

As time goes on, the technology skills will of course need to be revised. The definitive list of what your staff needs to know is a moving target—it likely changes every month or two as new technologies, resources, and services are introduced. The overall climate for what staff need to know will be in constant flux. My recommendation for dealing with this inevitability is to reconvene the skills taskforce once a year to review and maintain the skills plus any time a significant new technology resource or service is introduced that will require new skills. Libraries that find their technology moving very slowly may want to opt for a biannual revision schedule.

New skills should be approved by the same process used for the original skills, going through various groups and individuals for final approval. When new skills are ready for staff to review, make sure to highlight or mark which skills are the new ones so that employees can easily assess what's new. A reassessment should definitely take place when the new skills are introduced.

▶ PRIORITIZE TRAINING

All libraries are short on time, and therefore need to prioritize which training happens first, which trainings get approved, and who gets time to get what training. Sadly, I do not have a magic formula for picking the right trainings for your library and your staff. However, there are five key elements to keep in mind as you decide where to dedicate staff time and the training budget. These will come in handy when writing the organizational technology training plan (as discussed in the next section).

1. **Customer demand**: Will the skills or information included in the training support the individual's ability to provide the library's customers (including users and current nonusers) with the services they want and need? Trainings on new services, popular existing services, and crucial day-to-day job skills have factors of a high customer demand. Trainings on services outside the library's budget constraints, specialized topics on rarely used library resources, and other low-demand topics are still *nice* to be able to offer staff as evidence of a dedication to continuous learning and service excellence, but do not reflect customer demand.

2. **Organizational goals**: Do the objectives of the training support the library's mission, strategic goals for that year, or the unit's specific goals? Will that person's new skills help the library to develop its services, bring a valuable new service idea and information into the library, or in any other way support the library's aspirations?

3. **Immediate return on investment**: How long is the class? Does the class require travel time, or is it on-site or online? Does the training cost the library a fee? Does the class size allow for individual attention and specific questions to be answered? Is the topic something that is used every day by that staff member? Is the information easily relayed to other staff through the train-the-trainer model?

4. **Training effectiveness**: Is the instructor reputable or someone others have taken classes from before? Is the class in person or online? Is the format a lecture, small group work, hands-on, or another format? How is the material being presented best learned by the individual requesting the training? Is this the only opportunity for the training, or is the training offered in another format, time, or by someone else in a way that is more advantageous to the library?

5. **Consequences of a lack of training**: If the staff member does not attend the training, what are the consequences? Will their personal performance suffer or languish? Will their team suffer as a whole? Will the customer suffer?

▶ CREATE AN ORGANIZATIONAL TECHNOLOGY TRAINING PLAN

All organizations can benefit from a written technology training plan. Such a plan can assist library management (or the training coordinator) in every aspect of the staff training process. In the short term, the plan will help the library effectively spend training time and money wisely. In the long term, the plan will help the library staff members increase their skill level, knowledge, service delivery, and efficiency in a way that is noticeable throughout the institution.

Whenever I mention the word "plan" in a presentation or meeting, I get two looks: the glazed-over look that means "oh, that's nice but I sure as heck am not working on it" and the wide-eyed eyebrows-raised look that means "oh man, that is going to be a lot of work and I don't know how to do it." The reality is, though, that planning can be as simple or as complex as you want it to be. A work plan can be half a page of bullet points. It can be a two-paged table. Or, if the project is huge and you are an ambitious person who works overtime without getting paid, it can be a 60-page thesis on the process. My advice is to start simple; if you need to get more detailed, you'll know it. Be sure to include these simple steps in your written technology training plan:

▶ **Create a purpose statement**. Why is staff technology training important to the library? How does it support the mission?

▶ **Assess the staff's current skills**. How will the library assess staff, and on what skills? Who is creating the assessment? Who is evaluating the outcomes? Based on the assessment, what areas will require global attention? Which areas require fewer, or specialized, trainings? Once the assessment takes place, where are staff skills at on the whole? What type of training needs exist, and for how many, and which, people?

▶ **Evaluate the library's current learning environment overall**. How are staff receiving training now? How is training funding distributed? Are there required trainings for all staff? Are there mandated "continuing education credits" each year for librarians? For more help on evaluating your library's learning environment, take a look at TechAtlas (www.techatlas.org), a powerful technology planning tool free of charge to libraries courtesy of WebJunction.

TechAtlas covers more than just staff technology training (and it would benefit you to use those as well), but for now begin with its section on "Staff Professional Development Assessment." Through a series of questions about current funding, staff training attendance, internal offerings, needs, barriers, and your internal learning culture, you will be provided with a list of recommendations.

▶ **Create goals.** What does the library wish to achieve through technology training? What short- and long-term outcomes are desirable? Within each goal, create a set of objectives as well (shorter-term achievements that further your progress toward the goal).

Objectives can sometimes be tricky, so, if you find yourself stuck, remember the SMART acronym for creating successful objectives: Specific, Measurable, Achievable, Realistic, and Time-bound. By incorporating these elements in your objectives, you will create stepping stones toward your goals that are concrete measurements of the program's progress.

▶ **Budget for training**. Through assessing staff needs, determining appropriate training options, and examining the staff training budget, the library may learn that it needs to dedicate more resources to staff training—both in staff hours (for the person receiving the training and his or her substitute if necessary) and in cash for purchasing off-site training.

▶ **Provide learning opportunities**. Who will coordinate training—an individual or a team? What trainings are already available through internal or partner organizations? What trainings are available through library Web sites like WebJunction and OPAL or through quality, reviewed, free technology tutorial Web sites? Where are the gaps? Who will offer what trainings, when, to whom, for how many people at a time, and where? What training methods are effective for what topics? What software and hardware needs will this create? How many staffing hours will be needed?

▶ **Evaluate the program**. Using the SMART-created objectives and their larger associated goals, where is the library six months after implementation? One year? How will you reassess and re-tool the program to meet ongoing and new needs?

▶ CREATE A STAFF LEARNING AND INNOVATION PLAN

Beyond the organizational technology training plan, each employee should receive a staff learning and innovation plan (SLIP). This plan will use the data that document where staff skills are currently (focusing specifically on technology or looking at a wider set of staff skills). The plan needs to reflect the goals set by the organization and the staff member and determine how to meet those goals through learning opportunities. Call it whatever you like, but do emphasize "learning" over "teaching," and "innovation" over "competence." We want our staff to learn and to use that learning to help the library innovate on a continual basis. This is where the "innovation" comes in—staff training is not all about meeting the bare minimum requirements. Staff training in libraries is about constantly improving, looking at the world around us, at our communities, and figuring out what we can do to give them the best access to information and learning opportunities themselves.

Each SLIP can be very short and simple (one page should do it). It should include three elements:

1. Skill areas where the organization and/or the staff member would like to see development
2. Training opportunities, either internal or external, that the staff member and the supervisor feel would help meet these goals
3. A timeline for meeting these goals, including a priority list of which learning opportunities are most important

SLIPs should be created collaboratively with the library staff member and the supervisor working together. Bring in the help of the library's training expert, if you are lucky enough to have one, or specialists in the areas of learning—such as asking IT staff to suggest a basic networking class or asking the reference specialist to suggest fabulous readers' advisory resources. SLIPs should also be revised at least annually, and both staff members and supervisors should always feel welcome to add new learning priorities to a SLIP, making it a living document. The best success is likely to occur if libraries make the SLIP goals part of the employee's annual performance review. Learning is a priority for us and should be reflected in how we evaluate our staff success.

This may seem on the surface to be an overly simplistic approach to building training plans for your library and the staff. I can say from experience that the simpler the plan, the simpler the process for its creation, the sooner it will be implemented and the greater the chance for success. Ask staff to do A, B, and C and give them a valid reason to do it. It will be done. On the other hand, focusing on the bureaucratic processes, how to design the forms, and wordsmithing the document to death will indeed create dead documents—plans that sit on the intranet somewhere but are not used day to day to help the library and the staff evolve. If ever you needed a reason to keep it simple, here it is. Learning doesn't happen through bureaucratic processes—it happens through experiences, stories, and interest in improvement. If you want the organization to indeed be a learning organization, skip the paper-pushing and get directly to the learning.

▶ PROVIDE EFFECTIVE TECHNOLOGY TRAINING

Technology training is hard. Personally, I think it's the hardest type of training to do as it involves not only the people factors but also the uncontrollable technology itself. Add to these the general fear that many people have about figuring out new technologies (or even resentment) and you have a formula for a difficult experience. But it can be easy if you prepare in advance and keep some basic tips in mind. Nearly everything covered in this chapter applies to technology training for any group of people—library staff, students, members of the public, businesspeople . . . anyone! This chapter will also help you with the two Ds in our ADDIE training model: "Design" and "Development."

Creating effective technology training takes practice, time, and lots of mistakes along the way. However, by following the guidance of those who have made these mistakes before you, you are much more likely to succeed earlier in your life as a trainer. Respected expert trainer Brenda Hough (2006: 9–12) offers eight tips for technology trainers:

1. Stop trying to provide step-by-step directions.
2. Encourage independence.
3. Expect success.
4. Encourage exploration.
5. Provide context.
6. Treat training as a collaborative project.
7. Use storytelling.
8. Be real-world.

Two other experienced trainers, Rachel Singer Gordon and Michael Stephens (2006: 34–35), offer up ten tips of their own:

1. Carry multiple versions of your training documents, both digitally and in hard copy.
2. Use real-world examples for exercises.
3. Create an online community around your training.
4. Use audio/visual and hands-on tools.
5. Create how-to handouts and more with PowerPoint.
6. Promote classes with Flickr.
7. Keep up-to-date with online resources.
8. Rehearse a bit, but go with the flow.
9. Take a look at Web 2.0 tools and start playing.
10. Enjoy what you do!

Technology training authority Stephanie Gerding provides wonderful checklists helpful for planning effective technology training, a "Preparation Checklist" and "10 Tips for Preparation" (Gerding, 2007: 156–157). If you are at all uncomfortable preparing for training sessions or making sure you remember all of the details on your way to a class, take a look at her lists.

Creating Materials

Some of the classes for your staff will require you to create original materials. This will usually happen in cases where the topic is specific to procedures internal to your library or for software (like your ILS) for which the vendor has provided inadequate, or no, training materials. The best practices discussed will help you create the finest possible training materials, but can also be used when evaluating materials created by others for your staff. Also keep in mind that many of the handouts or other materials you create for staff technology training are likely going to be useful as is, or with slight modifications, for training your library customers. That's two for one!

Organizing and Formatting Materials Effectively

All training materials need to follow the basic principles of the following five categories for success:

1. **Visual clarity**: Use a simple, easy-to-read, large font; contrast between background and text/images; clearly delineate headings and sections; use high-resolution, clear images; provide text boxes or shaded areas with special tips and techniques; keep the text on slides to a minimum—slides should include five or less bulleted points and have plenty of space between the points.

2. **Organization**: Overall, attempt to organize the materials from the perspective of a new learner. Include positive outcomes of learning the subject being taught, key discussion points or step-by-step instructions if necessary, and resources for more information.

3. **Detail**: Leave things as simple as possible, infusing detail (such as step-by-step instructions) only when necessary to the level of absorption you expect from the learners.

4. **Screenshots**: Many trainers have abandoned screenshots entirely. Instead, include images of only the relevant button, search box, or toolbar—and only when absolutely necessary to help the learners absorb the process.

5. **Templates**: Consider creating training material templates to be used for all classes; a consistency in format will help trainers create materials quicker and help learners with a recognizable format for each class.

Using Stand-Alone Materials

Sometimes a topic is effectively learned through stand-alone materials given to each learner to go through at his or her own pace. If materials you are creating are meant to stand on their own, without instructor assistance, the materials have to be a bit more perfect than the other materials. Remember to include all of those things that you might mention in a class, including items like tips and tricks. Stand-alone materials are one of the few places that I recommend including step-by-step instructions for processes. The students don't have you there with them to lead them through the process, so the materials need to stand on their own. Pay a lot of attention to every aspect of the materials. Better yet, ask a colleague to walk through the materials as a practice step to catch anything that is missing or confusing.

Using Materials During the Classes

First off, anytime you are creating materials for an in-person or even live online class, be sure to include an agenda. This lets learners know what to expect, and when, including breaks. Learners come to trainings expecting to get good information, but usually they also come expecting to have materials to follow during the class. There are many learners who feel more comfortable having something to look at in front of them, such as slide handouts, instead of looking at the slides on the screen. This allows them to take notes, follow along at their own pace, and know that they will come away with something after the class.

Make sure to pass out *all* handouts at the start of any class, or in the case of online materials, to make them available for access before the class. Do not wait until that specific handout is needed, because distribution at that point disrupts the flow of the class, does not give learners an organized packet of materials, and actually may *prevent* some learners from getting the most out of the class. The desire to withhold handouts until needed is driven by the dislike some instructors have for the "read-ahead" learners. Some will choose to read ahead, yes, but this is usually because they are bored with the material currently being presented and have decided that the best use of their time is to read ahead and learn instead of tuning out or listening to information they already know. This is a good thing. Our learners are adults—let us treat them like adults and let them decide when they want to access our supporting materials.

Using Online Materials

Many trainers are accustomed to using print materials. Using online materials, however, allows for increased access, flexibility, and environmental consciousness. Some instructors keep it simple by posting their slides and other supporting materials on the library's intranet and pointing students to the links. You can also post presentations and handouts to free sites like Slideshare or Google Docs. Other instructors take it a step further by actually creating the materials in an online environment, such as through blog posts or a wiki devoted to that specific class. Creating a site that is dedicated to an individual class is particularly effective for classes about Web services and resources, as the students are using the environment that they are learning about. Consider creating a class wiki and distributing the URL for the class ahead of time. Ask students to post their questions (what they want to learn) ahead of time. Post any handouts or slides to the site, and ask students to print out copies for themselves before the class. This way you don't end up with extraneous copies that end up in the recycling bin.

Making Materials Useful After the Class

As mentioned earlier, include a list of resources and materials for use in the workplace after the training. This can include articles, tutorials, Web sites, blog posts, and even additional materials the library has created on related subjects. Students who are motivated to continue the learning process can do so, and those who want to delve into a specific aspect of the training topic can do so with the materials you provide them. What better way to encourage continuous learning? Finally, include contact information for the instructor or anyone else who supports the topic being presented. This gives learners a place to turn with questions or frustrations.

Making Materials Fun

For the life of me, I don't know why, but library folks are generally pretty dry in their writing and presenting. Loosen up, library nation! Use fun and casual language in your materials—not institution-speak. You even have permission to make some tasteful jokes. Use humorous real-world examples from library life, which we know has plenty of material for jesting. When presenting steps for an effective reference interview, try using amusing real-world examples, such as requests for information on the "electrical college and voting" or "photographs of George Washington, preferably in color." Also throw in some outside-the-library examples to loosen things up. If teaching how to comment on a blog, for example, show a blog that is light-hearted, such as Pet Holdings' Lolcats blog (http://icanhascheezburger.com) showing cat photos with hilarious captions with bad grammar and spelling. Ask the class to pick one of the posts from the last week and leave a comment. They'll learn commenting in a hands-on way and on a fun site that they will likely remember better than a boring test blog created for the class.

Keeping Classes and Workshops Comfortable

Holding a traditional icebreaker activity will help only a few of your learners and likely irritate or even alienate the others. There is definitely a benefit to starting the class off with something informal as a way to ease learners into the learning environment and introduce them to those around them they may not know. Few icebreaker activities, in my experience, have been what I would call "fun," but these activities seem to work better than most:

▶ **"Last" Introductions**: Ask all class members to introduce themselves with standard information (name, position, location) but also ask what they hope to get out of the class, and ask each person to answer the same question (which should vary from class to class), such as the last movie they saw, the last person they read e-mail from, the last book they read, the last place they visited, etc.

▶ **Truth or Lies**: All class members stand and state one thing about themselves that is true, and one that is a lie. The class has to guess which is which.

▶ **Scavenger Hunt**: Create a list of interesting facts like "loves sushi," "drinks coffee every day," "belongs to a community organization," etc. Ask students to find someone who fits each category by roaming the room and talking with others.

▶ **Art-i-fact**: Distribute blank pieces of paper and drawing materials, and ask everyone to draw the three things they would put in a time capsule to represent the library.

To create an interesting learning environment, I also recommend playing music before the class, during breaks, and perhaps even during the class, but only if it is slow, without lyrics, and unobtrusive. You can use streaming online audio from sites like Pandora or Last.fm or your own choices through MP3s on your computer or through an iPod docking station.

Providing Interactive Learning Experiences

Learning studies over the past century have shown that people learn in different ways. Most people learn best from interactive learning, from hands-on interaction, or from discussions and other interactions with instructors and students. Few people learn best from a straight lecture format. My own favorite classes as a student are relatively smallish groups where the class structure is quite varied: short lecture or demo followed by individual or small group exercises, small group discussions, whole group discussions, and group Q&A sessions. I generally recommend a ratio of one part lecture to two parts interactive practice or discussion.

One of the interactive options that I use frequently is role playing as a way to teach what to do and what not to do. Write out a basic script and call for a volunteer from the audience. For example, create a script to teach how not to upload photos to Flickr. You could start with, "Oh, I have 397 photos on my camera. I'll upload them all directly to Flickr without any editing, weeding, or re-naming of the files. And better yet, I won't bother to add any titles, tags, or descriptions. Ha!" Adding a bit of humor and class participation will help students to retain the information longer and make the class fun at the same time.

For an extensive list of suggestions on how to make your class interactive, see Stephanie Gerding's (2007: 74–82) examples of interactive learning exercises in Chapter 5 of her superb book *The Accidental Technology Trainer: A Guide for Libraries.*

Distinguishing Computer and Noncomputer Learning

How one teaches has a lot to do with whether the subject is computer based. By necessity, many topics on which library staff require training today involve the use of computer hardware and software. While the essential principles of training apply no matter what you are teaching or how, there are some key concepts for successfully training using a computer:

▶ **Keep your hands to yourself**: Let the student do all the typing and mousing. This is how students learn best.

▶ **Keep your eyes on them**: Stay at the physical level of the computer users, especially when working one on one. Sit in a chair or squat down (if your knees are better than mine) so as to create an equitable symbolic power structure. Look at the student when he or she looks at you, and look at the computer when he or she does.

▶ **Be extra patient**: This applies for all topics, but it's somehow easier for instructors to get impatient and students to get frustrated with the introduction of the wicked computer into the training formula.

▶ **Classrooms need screens**: If working in a computer classroom and instructing a group of people, you will find it much easier if you have an instructor's computer at the front of the class and are able to project what you see to the front of the classroom. This will allow students to follow along on your screen if they have gotten lost on their own.

Pacing and Timing

Many new instructors make the mistake of jumping right into the subject matter and plowing straight through until the end of the class. Best practices for pacing and timing in classes include the following, all things that you likely appreciate when you are attending a class as a student yourself:

▶ **Honor the biological clock**. No, not *that* biological clock. Everyone's energy clock is different, but most people naturally get tired after lunch. Early afternoon classes tend to have sleepier learners who will participate and retain less. Midmorning and late afternoon sessions work best in my opinion. If the class is a half or a full day and you can't control the scheduling, you can still be mindful of people's tired-meters. Don't rely on your own level of tiredness as a meter, though, because instructors seem to achieve a pseudo-adrenaline high when teaching and have all the energy in the world while in front of the class, and soon collapse after the class is done. I haven't quite figured out the cause for this yet, so if anyone has, let me know.

▶ **Begin on time**. I have discovered that in my over 300 classes, my mind is made up differently each time about when to begin. I had one class where over half the class arrived over half an hour late. I nearly had an aneurism 15 minutes after the start time and I was still waiting—and so were my on-time students. I learned an important lesson then, and adjusted my practice. My general rule is that I begin on time. I remind people of this in the reminder e-mail before the training. If less than three-fourths of the class is present at the time we are set to start, however, I will wait five additional minutes and let the class know we'll start in five, to inform the people who did arrive on time and give them the chance to run to the bathroom or get a coffee. But, in truth, each class is different.

▶ **Have breaks**. If the class is one hour or more in length, provide breaks. My general rule is that for every hour, students should have ten minutes to stretch, use the restroom, and rest. Mark the beginning and end of breaks with bells (I have some lovely meditation chimes that I try to use). More students will come back on time if you tell them at what precise time the break will end instead of simply stating that they have ten minutes to break.

▶ **Have a flexible timeline**. After reviewing the agenda at the beginning of the class, give the class about one minute to review the agenda (written somewhere hopefully) and to suggest any changes that they think would make the class better. Take students' suggestions, but be careful to not let students with a particular issue change the entire class to focus on their own narrow agenda.

▶ **Ramp up and ramp down**. Ease into the subject matter with some quick and easy discussions and exercises. Place the difficult and core material toward the middle of the class, and then provide a sort of wind-down in the last 15 minutes or so of the class where students can review what they have learned and ask any lingering questions.

Encouraging Participation

Learners who do not participate are a much more common occurrence than most new trainers would think. There are a number of techniques for encouraging everyone to participate appropriately. Here are some of the methods that have worked the best for me:

▶ **Ask questions instead of giving answers**. When asked a question by a student for which the answer is opinion based or has multiple right answers, throw the question back at the class. This will let people shine and will create more opportunities for everyone in the class to contribute their opinions.

▶ **Collaborate**. Work together with learners throughout the class instead of simply talking at them. If you set up an atmosphere immediately involving students in each conversation, and making the dispersion of knowledge less unidirectional, more students will feel comfortable participating and giving their opinions.

▶ **Be encouraging and supportive**. Many people withdraw and fail to participate in classes when they feel that the instructor is harsh, uninterested in them or the topic, and ego driven. Be as encouraging of each participant as you can, and support everyone's contributions, even when incorrect or misleading. Redirect the conversation where you want it to go but never at the expense of humiliating or alienating a learner. A great way to gain the trust of learners is to encourage them, at the start of the class, to give you feedback throughout the session—whether you are going too quickly or too slow, if something needs repeating, if everyone there knows a particular concept already, etc. Learners will remember your support and the trust you had in their abilities, which will translate into confidence in their newfound skills.

▶ **Stop periodically for questions**. After each new concept, ask if there are questions. Encourage students to give you feedback about the class, too—to tell you if you are going too quickly or too slowly. Count to ten in your head, giving people time to think about and formulate their questions or feedback, and if no one speaks by "ten," then it's time to proceed.

▶ **Do not touch the keyboard or mouse**. The students need to learn how to do the task. Under no circumstances should an instructor take control of a student's mouse or keyboard in order to move through something more quickly or even to try to "teach" (trust me—you're not teaching anyone anything).

Encouraging Retention

There is a big difference between teaching and training—training is interactive, inclusive of learners' individual needs, and results in better retention of information. When acting as an instructor for any class, for staff or not, remember that your learners likely do not need to learn the theory behind the subject. They have come to learn what is necessary for their lives and what is practical: how to do the task, how to gain from the task, how to practice, and how to follow up and share the information with others in their work group who will also benefit from the information.

Also, remember that this information may be old hat to you, but it is completely new to your learners. No one is born knowing how to use software or provide good customer service. Unfortunately, most trainers have forgotten what it is like to be a beginner. Try to remember, because the more you can do that the more you will connect with your learners and help them learn.

It is also key to watch for that saturation point at which you can see students' eyes glaze over with what I call the "undergraduate lecture hall look." If learners begin looking around instead of at you, chatting with each other instead of listening, or even falling asleep, this is probably a good signal that you have lost the class, likely due to being overloaded with information (it's either that or boredom, and let's hope it's not the latter). If you see this happen, take an unscheduled break and then come back and ask how everyone is feeling. Ideally, they will be ready for more information.

Use real-world and personal examples to connect what is being taught with some other information or interest already in your learner's mind. The connections made in the brain will be more solid if this technique is used. For example, show real-world examples of other libraries or institutions successfully using what you are teaching. Show ways to use what you are teaching in the real-life situations in the library; an easy way to do this is to ask students for ways they think the topic could benefit them and also following up on any learning goals communicated to you at the beginning of the class. Using personal examples, completely unrelated to the library (yes, this is allowed), allows students to follow their own interests (such as quilting or Taiko drumming). If you can find a way to fold personal interests into the class's topic, not only will students perk up and pay close attention, they will also remember the subject matter much easier.

Finally, remember to highlight some of the tips and tricks that seem simple to you. There are buttons, toolbar options, keyboard shortcuts, and menu choices that many staff members have never experimented with or used. Some of my students comment that they most love the tips and tricks for the easy things, instead of the more advanced processes that the class is supposed to cover.

▶3

IMPLEMENTATION

▶ **Develop a Basic Staff Technology Training Program**

▶ **Run a Lunchtime Brown Bag Training Session**

▶ **Form a Peer Training Program**

▶ **Create a Train-the-Trainer Program**

▶ **Develop a 23 Things Course**

▶ **Develop a Technology Petting Zoo**

▶ **Utilize Online Training Sources**

This chapter includes a how-to for several types of technology training programs. Each section includes easy-to-follow steps and important tips.

▶ DEVELOP A BASIC STAFF TECHNOLOGY TRAINING PROGRAM

We have now made it to the letter I in our ADDIE training model: "Implementation." What do we do next? What kind of training program will work best for your staff? Start with the fundamentals. Creating a basic technology training program is a wonderful first step for any library attempting to help its staff members increase their technology skills. A basic program generally includes a series of in-person classes, online materials, and other directly provided trainings. Most basic technology training programs include a somewhat organized approach to the classes—driven either by a staff technology skills appraisal or by institutional goals and position descriptions. In addition, most include a training coordinator, be it an individual or a committee. With any staff technology training program, the following issues are key for success.

Topics for Basic Technology Training Programs

If your institution has not yet begun preparations for any kind of coordinated technology training, then a basic program is a wonderful place to start. And because a "basic" program can include pretty much anything you want, it is infinitely flexible and moldable to any library's unique needs. The topics that work well for a basic technology training program are primarily defined by the current and desired skill levels of the library staff.

There are a number of techniques to identify current and desired staff skill levels, thereby identifying key training topics. For more information and details on doing this effectively, see "Develop a Technology Skills List" in Chapter 2. Typically, basic technology training programs begin with the most basic topics in order to develop skills sequentially for staff who need the most training. Basic topics include simple computer skills, printer troubleshooting, Web browser navigation, e-mail usage, and directing patrons to the library's Web content.

Training Types

Basic training programs usually involve a limited number of in-person trainings on the most essential topics. These can be taught by in-library experts, training staff, people in the parent institutions, or other local training resources (such as California's statewide library training organization, Infopeople). The key here is to not get too ambitious. If you are starting off with no existing organized program, taking small steps and ensuring the success of short-term training goals is more important than creating an extensive program or an exhaustive catalog of great online library training resources. The essence of any basic training program is to get library staff what they need immediately and then move on from there.

Scheduling and Location Issues

With any in-person trainings, there are scheduling issues. It is important when planning for the trainings to ensure that staff have advanced notice so they can plan to attend and that the data and time works for as many staff as possible. I have found that scheduling classes to start on the half-hour (e.g., 2:30) works best as it gives people a half-hour to get from their location to the training location, if necessary, which apparently is more desirable for those scheduling service points. The location should be easily accessible by all staff, and it should be as comfortable as possible. Make certain that any technology needs are met ahead of time in the location of the class, including hardware, software, and network access.

Another issue is scheduling classes in relation to other classes. Be sure to schedule classes with some time in between so that not every single class for the quarter is offered the same week. Also try to schedule classes on an ongoing and rotating basis. Don't train on blogs once, and then throw away the key to that class. Train on blogs, then Flickr, then Excel, then troubleshooting skills, yadda yadda, then eventually back to the beginning again and back to blogs. Of course, you have to evaluate your "class line-up" on an ongoing basis to ensure that the classes are still relevant and that you're not missing anything.

Online trainings offer their own challenges, including the fact that many managers forget or do not want to schedule time off of library service points for staff to participate in online training, especially if it is not live online training (such as an asynchronous self-paced class). Work with managers to guarantee equitable systemwide promotion and support of online trainings if the basic technology training program includes online elements. As I always say to our library staff members: "Online counts too!"

Staff Buy-In

People who want to learn, learn. People who don't want to learn, generally don't. Convincing staff that it is in their best interest to gain technology skills can be a daunting and seemingly impossible task. I strongly believe that nearly every potential learner can find a reason to be invested in technology training. It's just a matter of finding each individual's motivation. And hopefully we can find some internal motivation for each student (wanting to increase one's confidence) as opposed to external motivation (fear of a bad evaluation). Internal motivation tends to yield better results and create a more enjoyable learning experience.

Carolyn M. Gray (1983: 72) drove home the importance of staff buy-in when she said:

> Without early involvement of the people affected by the technological changes in the planning process, we set ourselves up for failure. We are talking about more than minimal levels of competencies needed to perform functions; we are talking about attitudes, resistance to change and more.

The following list includes some tried and true ways to get staff buy-in. Some techniques may work better for each individual library's staffing, political, and cultural situation:

- ▶ **Hold brainstorming sessions**: People love to talk, so encourage them to do so! Hold open brainstorming sessions as described in Chapter 2's section on creating skills lists.

- ▶ **Survey staff**: Create a survey for staff asking them either what they feel they need training on or what trainings they would actually attend. For more on surveys, see Chapter 2's section on creating skills lists.

- ▶ **Keep staff informed**: Nothing spells disaster for any project, especially one laden with change for staff, as quickly as a lack of information and communication about the project. Keep staff informed at all times about the purpose of the training program, available trainings, survey outcomes, skill improvements, and anything else related to the technology training program. Employ whatever communication mechanisms reach the most people—e-mail, staff newsletter entries, committee meeting discussions, etc. Giving staff information builds trust between those coordinating the technology trainings and the staff at large.

Management Buy-In

Beyond achieving general staff buy-in, getting managers to accept and promote the training program is sometimes difficult, but essential. I have my own acronym that I use whenever faced with difficulties in getting managers to understand what I believe will work for the library, or trying to get the management to approve a project. For some reason, keeping these four simple things in mind helps me to stay composed and approach each situation calmly. So, think **G-R-O-W**—**G**oals, **R**eality, **O**ptions, **W**ay forward:

Goals—What is the project trying to achieve? Who are you attempting to affect? How will this benefit library users and/or library staff?

Reality—Putting the "pie in the sky" ideal world aside for a moment, what is the real situation in terms of budget, local rules and regulations, time, etc.?

Options—Consider the goals and reality, and come up with a few different approaches that can be presented to managers so that they feel they are in control. This is a classic "managing your manager" technique—instead of only presenting your ideal approach, present some other less desirable choices as well (sometimes *so* undesirable that managers will choose your approach automatically).

Way forward—When presenting your idea, include a short "what's next" section outlining the next few steps and how long each should take. This helps management understand exactly what to expect as a follow-up.

Here are a few more specific techniques to increase the chances of managers buying in to the training program:

▶ Attend a managers' meeting to formally discuss the technology training program, including the importance of specific technologies in the library and the positive customer service impact of tech-savvy staff.

▶ It doesn't hurt to show the competition, either—find other libraries with tech training programs and get positive quotes from articles or from them directly. Present statistics about staff's current skill levels and/or desire for training (depending on what you surveyed or tested).

▶ Finally, managers are ultimately beholden to their users. Talk directly and in simple language about how the new technology and resulting staff skills will benefit the managers' communities of users, be it through more high-quality customer service, an increase in staff-provided computer classes, or whatever else it is that their community demands.

Resistant Learners' Buy-In

Resistant learners (individuals who resist a particular learning topic or all topics) are one of the hardest groups to deal with in a training environment. However, there is one tried and true way to encourage resistant learners to re-think their position: *Show them why they should care.* The apathy and hostility that resistant learners usually present to trainers generally stems from a feeling that this new "thing" does not apply to them or is not worth their time to learn. Find out what the resistant learner is interested in, be it in the work environment or in personal life. Maybe it is cooking or baseball, or maybe even antique cameras. Whatever it is that they are interested in, spend 30–60 minutes with the person in a one-on-one session showing him or her how the technology bene-fits the library but also how it ties in to his or her own interests. Find blogs on the topic to teach blogging or RSS. Find photos and Flickr groups, discussion boards, podcasts, whatever it might be. In most cases, the resistant learner will turn into an eager participant overnight.

However, there are some learners who are resistant to all learn-ing due to personal disinterest, disagreement with the library's pri-orities, or the ever-popular excuse, "I'm retiring in five years—I'm not learning anything new!" Dealing with these resistant learners requires the involvement of the supervisor and trying to discover the reason behind the resistance. In some cases it may even re-quire enforcing negative consequences for not learning. These cases are few and far between, thankfully, but relying on existing personnel policies is the only solution in these situations.

Generational Differences

Libraries are certainly multigenerational work environments. A common mistake in teaching technology is to make generational assumptions—"Everyone under 35 is a technical genius, and every-one over 35 is an unskilled technophobe." While those on your staff who are digital natives may have a higher percentage of technology skills overall, the key principle to remember is that all staff need to be treated equally when it comes to expectations and learning opportunities. Different generations of workers do display different work and learning styles, however, and remembering these potential differences is vital to successful technology training. Institutions and trainers who accommodate, not ignore, different learning styles can turn generational obstacles into opportunities.

Traditionalists (born 1900–1945) respect the traditional chain of command in the workplace, are highly dedicated, and believe the place of the employee is to constantly prove himself or herself to those in command. *Baby Boomers* (born 1946–1964) require recognition from higher ups and expect to succeed in the workplace through hard work and loyalty. *Generation X* (born 1965–1980) are cynical, self-sufficient, believe loyalty has to be earned, and generally do not trust those in power until they have proven themselves to be trustworthy. *The Millennials* (born 1980–1999) are organizationally and team driven, trust authority, and require meaningful work and constant feedback on their performance.

So, what does all of this mean for learning styles and effective technology training? Educational Psychology and Instructional Technology Professor Thomas C. Reeves (2007) believes that Traditionalists and Baby Boomers develop knowledge in a more structural and formal way, while younger generations tend to learn in an informal and nonhierarchical way. Some have attributed this to the increased amount of video game participation, particularly live online multiplayer games, by the younger generations. Despite a moderate number of articles and books about learning style differences among the generations, there are no research-based findings to substantiate any of the claimed differences and teaching techniques. Learning is apparently still learning, no matter how old the student! However, remember to always consider learners' values, some of which will be based on their generational experiences. Instructors will find success in training the different generations by remaining sensitive to what is important to learners, such as loyalty (Traditionalists), rewards for good work (Baby Boomers), the freedom to explore on their own (Generation X), and group dynamics (Generation Y). When all is said and done, every learner is ultimately unique and will find motivation in training opportunities in his or her own way. All we can do as training coordinators and instructors is provide the connections between the training topic and the individual's values.

Incentives versus Negative Consequences

Staff rewards and incentives can go a long way toward ensuring the measurable impact and success of the training program. And the success of the training program ultimately means the success of the library's services for its customers. For some staff, the opportunity to learn new skills is enough of an incentive. For those who require a little extra push, consider the following ideas.

Most annual employee evaluations require a rating or statement of job skill or training participation. Many staff members will be motivated to participate in a technology training program if such participation is being measured in a performance evaluation. Documenting topical training goals is an excellent way to motivate, and even simply remind, staff of their learning responsibilities (see the discussion of staff learning and innovation plans in Chapter 2); here are some ideas.

- ▶ Depending on the construction of the trainings, classes may be counted toward formal continuing education credits (which are required for some positions).
- ▶ Participation in the trainings program or measurable skill level improvement can be tied to pay increases or one-time bonuses.
- ▶ Participation in the training program can earn staff additional vacation hours or days. Every six hours of training could equate to an extra hour of paid vacation time.
- ▶ Skill level improvement can place staff at the top of the list for the next round of promotions.

Send out diplomas to those who complete classes. Numerous diploma templates can be found in word processing software and online, but I recommend the Diploma Generator (www.addletters .com/diploma-generator.htm). It's easy to create, simple to fill in, and looks pretty good when e-mailed or printed.

Purchase or seek donations (from businesses or even other staff) for small prizes. Staff can receive a small prize for participating and be entered into a larger raffle for completion, relative skill improvement, or some other equitable factor. The classic example of this model is the Public Library of Charlotte & Mecklenburg County (NC) Learning 2.0 Program, where participants received MP3 players and a laptop and a PDA were raffled off. It's amazing what people will do for a free pen, deck of cards, or temporary tattoo. Party stores, especially around Halloween, have some amazingly fun and interesting items for very little money, or you can look for deals online at stores like Kipp Toys (www.kipptoys.com). Some of my favorite rewards of those I've gotten are shown in Figure 3.1. Counterclockwise from upper left are a customized T-shirt, a plastic tiara, a glowing keychain, a USB cell phone charger with adaptors, and a deck of playing cards with images of

▶ Figure 3.1: Some of My Favorite "Little Gifts"

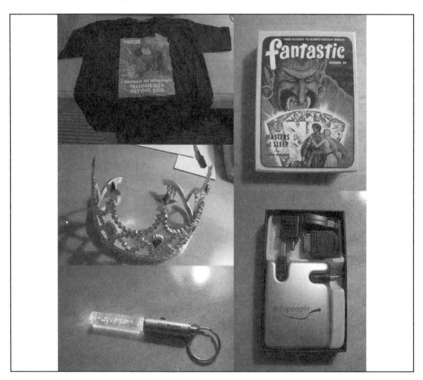

L. Ron Hubbard pulp fiction titles. I'm not too proud to admit that the tiara is my favorite and incidentally the cheapest.

Also remember that people love to collect sets of things, so, as you look at toys, buttons, prizes, or customized gear to give to your staff, ask yourself, "Can I make this into a collecting game?" If so, you just found one more way to help motivate staff to continue participating and learning.

Can't do any of these because of union or institutional rules? You're not alone, sadly. Many government agencies have policies against "rewarding" staff for doing their jobs or for soliciting donations from local businesses because this can be seen as endorsement and favoritism. What's a trainer to do? See what else is valued by your employees. Perhaps it is first dibs on desk hours. Or maybe it's working one less Saturday, getting a better desk chair, being at the top of the list for the new staff computers, having their very own donor bookplate in the library book of their choice, etc. There is always something that people want.

Unfortunately, and as much as we would like it to be untrue, not every library employee will be motivated and/or able to learn the skills required to do the job. This is particularly true of new technology skills and knowledge, because technology is an area some staff fear to learn and others feel they should not have to learn. Staff members must be accountable if they do not meet the skill levels required to do their jobs. This creates an extremely uncomfortable and unfortunate situation for all involved, but it is necessary for the overall health and progress of the institution.

When a staff member fails to participate in a needed and required training program, or participates and fails to absorb the skills over an adequate amount of time, the first step is to discover the reason. Perhaps the offered training was not at a good time, not offered through the best methodology for this particular learner, or at a level too advanced and therefore not absorbed. Or perhaps the learner attended the trainings multiple times but can simply not absorb the information. In the worst scenario, the staff member simply refuses to be trained. If the staff member is not participating or learning because of a fault in the trainings themselves, then the library is responsible and needs to find a way to address the learner's needs in the best way possible. The supervisor should set short-term goals that are both realistic and measurable for the employee and review the employee's performance regularly. By setting clear expectations, staying positive, and keeping these lines of communication open, the employee is likely to respond positively.

However, if the staff member is reluctant to be trained or simply cannot retain the information being presented, there need to be negative consequences for the employee. The consequences should be tailored to the situation and in keeping with existing institutional or union policies. Here are potential negative consequences frequently used in this type of scenario:

▶ Formal reprimand or documented discipline
▶ Poor ratings or negative comments in the employee's annual evaluation
▶ Position or location transfer to address lack of specific skills
▶ Demotion or reconfiguration of employee's position to address lack of skills
▶ Decrease in pay
▶ Termination

Many managers are more than happy to offer positive rewards for good performance but fail to address poor performance because it is unpleasant, requires confrontations, and often leads to unhappiness on the part of one or both parties. However, when poor performance is not addressed, the entire institution suffers, including that employee's immediate coworkers, the customers, and the reputation of the library in the community. If you find yourself or others wavering and not wanting to enforce any negative consequences for poor technology skill performance, I suggest reading (and rereading if necessary) the following quote from library technology training pioneer Anne Woodsworth (1997: 46):

> Incentives must be provided to encourage updating of selected competencies that are critical for the success of the library. These must include merit raises and/or promotions for those who succeed in changing and becoming technologically adept. Conversely, demotions or outright dismissal should be the con-

sequence for those who fail to become technologically competent.

Whatever the response from management, the consequences need to be consistent throughout the library and applied equitably to all staff members, regardless of how well they do other parts of the job, proximity to retirement, age, personality, gender, or any other irrelevant factors.

▶ RUN A LUNCHTIME BROWN BAG TRAINING SESSION

Lunchtime brown bag trainings typically consist of a short (one hour or less) in-person session, usually done in lecture or demonstration format, while the attendees eat a lunch, which they usually bring with them but may also be provided by the library. Brown bags can be held online as well, as a Webcast, while attendees lunch at their respective desks. Lunchtime brown bag trainings are a very popular method for two major reasons: (1) Brown bag trainings tend to be a little less formal than other training types and therefore more personalized. (2) Brown bags offer library staff with little time for training a way to combine lunch with learning. Many successful library training programs incorporate the lunchtime brown bag model, and technology training is one area in which this model can be quite effective. As you might imagine, holding a brown bag series for library customers can also be successful. Nearby customers can come over to the library for a 30-minute session during their lunch hours—an especially popular strategy if the library provides the sandwiches.

Topics for a Brown Bag Training Session

Because it is difficult to juggle food and a keyboard simultaneously, technology topics that do not require hands-on practice work best for the brown bag approach. Additionally, the limited amount of time available invites topics that can be covered quickly or dealt with in separate small chunks. Brown bags are fabulous for introducing new additions to existing services. Effective brown bags provide an overview or tour of the topic but do not go into extensive step-by-step procedures. Overall, the topic should be something that the learners can easily absorb without needing to take copious notes or wishing they had access to a computer to practice. Keep it simple, keep it quick, and keep it small. Here are some suggestions for successful library technology brown bag trainings:

▶ Individual Web tools (Google Docs, Jing, Flickr, etc.)

▶ Individual library databases

▶ New library catalog features

▶ Specific integrated library system features

▶ How to deal with information overload

▶ Basic overview of software applications or even specific tips within the applications (PowerPoint, Firefox, security software, etc.)

▶ How to stay up-to-date with libraries and technology

The University of Colorado (UC) at Boulder offers brown bag technology sessions for its staff on a variety of topics, including Microsoft Office, videoconferencing, graphic design, ergonomics, and much more (The Technology Topics Brown Bag Series, accessed 2009). The UC series has a substantial online presence, including a schedule of upcoming events, an archive of past events, training materials for each topic, and a recipe for the "dessert of the day" that the library provides at the event. Supplementing a brown bag session with online materials is an excellent way to extend the class's reach and to keep people interested. Plus, everyone loves food and recipes!

Speakers and Trainers

Fortunately, many brown bag sessions can be taught by your in-house talent. Staff members have a wide variety of skills in different areas, and each session can focus on one specific skill. When starting a brown bag series, it is a good idea to have experienced trainers or speakers present the first few sessions. At that point, begin recruiting staff to train on topics of interest to them. Keeping the trainings informal, somewhat like a one-on-one walk-through, helps new trainers to feel less intimidated by the prospect of training their coworkers. It may also be wise to recruit specialized trainers and speakers from outside your immediate organization, perhaps through your parent organization (city, school, university, etc.) or in the community.

Scheduling and Location

Scheduling a brown bag is easy—lunchtime! Most people hold one-hour sessions, but, depending on your library's lunch hour norms, you may only have 30 minutes for the session. Generally, I prefer to hold a session for 45 minutes, giving people an extra 15 minutes to socialize after the training is over. Ensure that the location is one that is central to your attendees, has comfortable chairs and tables, and is not a computer lab (Pellegrino and monitors don't mix!). Meeting rooms work particularly well. If the topic requires a computer demonstration, make certain that you have easy access to a laptop and projector at the front of the room, as well as a wireless or wired Internet connection if required. Remember— attendance at brown bags will vary greatly from one session to the next as interest and availability of the students waxes and wanes. If the room is limited in size, you may require sign-ups ahead of time. Ideally, though, the brown bags will be available on a drop-in basis, lending to the informal atmosphere of the training.

Legal and Union Issues

Some unions, human resources departments, and other organizational policies may prohibit employees from working during a lunch break. Training may or may not be considered working in your organization (although, in my humble opinion, training should always be considered working). As a result, some libraries may have to offer a brown bag forum in addition to a full lunch break and not as a replacement for the lunch break. Additionally, some libraries may be unable to require staff to attend trainings on a lunch hour, and others may even be unable to encourage such attendance. Check with your human resources and union policies to determine what your own library's requirements may be.

▶ FORM A PEER TRAINING PROGRAM

Peer training programs can be quite varied. Trainings can be on-line, in person, live, self-paced, short, long, detailed, and general. The one consistent factor is that the trainer is a staff member himself or herself, usually an on-the-job expert on the topic on which he or she is training.

Topics for Peer Training

Peer training can work for any topic, in theory, but it works especially well for topics that are used on the job regularly. The only topics to avoid are those that are potentially politically fraught (such as Internet filtering, the "right" way to do customer service). Political topics tend to result in personal viewpoints taking over the training and possible confrontations between trainer and students, which in a peer-to-peer environment can result in long-term discord between coworkers. Traditionally, peer training is set up as regular training is (e.g., a Monday 2–4 p.m. class on RSS feeds) but is also sometimes done on the spot. Much "new staff" training is done through peer training, whether by accident or by design. These are some potential topics to teach through peer training:

- ▶ Creating a new patron account
- ▶ Downloading an e-audiobook
- ▶ Posting meeting minutes to the library's intranet
- ▶ Conducting effective online reference interviews
- ▶ Using online chat reference software
- ▶ Using your e-mail account

Peer Trainers

First and foremost, peer trainers need to have the qualities of a good trainer. Of course, it helps if they are also experts on the subject of the training so that they can effectively answer their coworkers' questions. Overall, it is a lot easier to train someone on a specific skill than it is to train people on how to be good trainers, so choose your peer trainers predominantly because of their "trainer" qualities. If the library has people on staff who are good communicators, enthusiastic about the subject matter, patient, and flexible, then you have an excellent pool of potential peer trainers. Stephanie Gerding (2007: 53) provides an excellent list of qualities of a good technology trainer in her book *The Accidental Technology Trainer: A Guide for Libraries*:

> ▶ Being flexible and adaptive to difficult situations
> ▶ Having excellent presentation and communication skills
> ▶ Designing and delivering training that addresses all learning styles
> ▶ Knowing the content and keeping up-to-date on technology and training issues
> ▶ Being enthusiastic, engaging, and responsive to participants' ongoing needs
> ▶ Ensuring that learning occurs and effectively creating a learning community
> ▶ Modeling what is trained by example

I would also add the following three qualities:

> ▶ Having a customer-centered approach toward expanding people's access to and understanding of information
> ▶ Displaying honesty, even when it means admitting something you don't know
> ▶ Having patience with difficult people and situations

Teaching Others How to Train on Technology Topics

If the library has a great group of knowledgeable staff members who do not necessarily have technology training skills, all is not lost! It is still quite achievable to teach those staff members how to do effective technology training.

In the past I have found it useful to hold a "train-the-trainer" boot camp, where I train others on technology training best practices. The boot camp consists of a handful of sessions spread out over a few weeks. We generally start with an overview of training best practices, brainstorming on what each of us likes and dislikes in trainers, non-training communication practice sessions, training communication practice sessions, technology training development and teaching checklists, practice developing technology training materials, organization best practices, and other specialized sessions as necessary.

A valuable way to get non-trainers comfortable and practiced with training is to have them work in teams and begin with team-taught trainings instead of individually taught trainings. This will help to teach the skills necessary, offer adequate practice, and at the same time offer needed training opportunities to the rest of the staff. It is helpful if an experienced trainer can observe the first few sessions from any new trainer and offer feedback so that the new trainer can further develop his or her skills.

Speaking Anxiety

Some new trainers (and experienced trainers too!) experience speaking anxiety. Staff who work with customers regularly tend to be more comfortable training, as they have practice dealing with different people in constantly changing situations, as well as speaking to strangers. Staff without customer contact may find the transition to trainer somewhat more difficult. The best way to get over any speaking or training nervousness is to practice, practice, practice. The more times you practice each presentation, and the more presentations you practice, the more comfortable you will be with any group. There are many opportunities to practice your speaking outside of the library if that feels like an easier first step. Toastmasters clubs are common in many communities and offer the chance to listen to others speak, speak yourself, and receive critiques. Many community colleges and adult learning centers offer public speaking opportunities, and there are a wealth of books, Web sites, and articles on the subject. In the end, though, you have to do it to learn it.

Strange as it is, before and during my own speaking and training gigs, I keep the following pneumonic device in mind to keep my nerves in check: **TRAIN—T**ics, **R**espect, **A**ir, **I**ntelligence, **N**otes:

Tics—Many of us have verbal tics, filler words that we rely on when we are nervous. Examples include "like," "umm," "you know," "right?," and "so." In all likelihood, you know what your verbal tics are. Be aware of them as you speak and attempt to quiet them.

Respect—Your class is made up of adults. Treat them with the same respect that you would wish as a student yourself. Pause and ask for questions. Listen to their opinions. And don't forget to respect their bodies, too! Allow time for stretch breaks and mingling.

Air—Air is essential while speaking. Think about your breathing. Feel the air come in, let the air go out. Many new speakers hyperventilate unintentionally because of nerves. If you begin to feel nervous, slow down your breathing and take two breaths in and out before continuing.

Intelligence—You know more about the subject than your audience does. That's why they're here—to hear what you know about the subject. Even if you don't think you know, pretend that you do. Faked confidence often looks the same as the real thing!

Notes—New trainers sometimes read an entire presentation from notecards or a PowerPoint screen. This is absolutely *not* what I am advocating. When the nerves hit full force, however, it is quite nice to have speaking notes to fall back on. When this happens, try to use your notes for one point or screen (to get your bearings back) and then go back to speaking without the notes, which sounds and looks more natural. Please, please, please do not use PowerPoint as cue cards. You will make your students cry.

▶ CREATE A TRAIN-THE-TRAINER PROGRAM

Train the trainer is a model to use when a large number of people need to learn about a particular topic, usually in a short time frame, and the available training resources are unable to reach every learner efficiently. Train the trainer offers an in-depth centralized class for a preselected set of learners (one person from each location or department, for example), who then take that training back to the staff at their location and offer the training themselves to that group. Train-the-trainer programs are common in most libraries, but are most widespread in large, multiple-location systems. Successful train-the-trainer programs help the institution as a whole to become more self-sufficient over time to deal more easily with staff turnover by spreading technology skills throughout the organization.

Topics for a Train-the-Trainer Program

When a library begins to offer a new service, the service vendor will often charge a fee for every person it has to train. At other times, an expensive or out-of-area class is held that would benefit the entire staff, but it is simply impossible to send the entire staff to the training. Therefore, topics tend to be quite varied. Here are some examples:

▶ Administering the public-use computer time-out software

▶ Using Dreamweaver to manage the library's Web site

▶ Learning advanced Microsoft SharePoint features

▶ Searching the invisible Web

Overall, whenever money and time are issues with training a large number of staff, consider sending only a handful of people to the official training and relying on your "trained trainers" to educate the rest of the staff.

A Successful Train-the-Trainer Program

The major pitfall in the train-the-trainer model is the heavy reliance on one individual to teach others. It is essential to ensure that the "trainer" is familiar with how to teach and train already so that when the new information is ready it can be effectively disseminated to the rest of the staff. Trainers need the skills listed earlier in the peer training section. In addition, because of the unique nature of the train-the-trainer model, they also need to know how to effectively take notes during the official training to share later with others. Technology topics are particularly thorny. If the official training does not offer good class materials, step-by-step note-taking becomes even more crucial.

Trainer Support

In both the train-the-trainer and peer training models, there should be a central source of support for all trainers, especially new trainers. These trainers need to have been taught the key principles of teaching, training, and facilitation. Patience, flexibility, and enthusiasm are always important for any technology trainer. Trainers need constant communication with a training coordinator or experienced trainer who can offer feedback on materials and presentation skills. Trainers may also find that they need assistance in putting together their class materials or even an assistant for teaching the class itself. Finally, trainers need easy access to materials and media required for training others, such as audiovisual equipment, the ability to reserve classrooms, a supply of markers and poster board, etc. When the institution has invested so much in a single person's knowledge on a particular topic, supporting that person with time and resources is especially critical to the institution's success.

If your library needs a little bit of help getting a program like this started, it would be of great benefit to hold a class for the "soon to be" trainers first about how to train effectively. Infopeople offers a wonderful day-long class titled "Train the Trainer," taking time to actually teach library staff to be great trainers (see http://infopeople .org/training/past/2004/train-trainer-gould/). The skills learned can help when training other staff or training the public. The course description Web site offers a detailed syllabus as well as information on arranging for a session at your own library.

▶ DEVELOP A 23 THINGS COURSE

In 2006, the ever-brilliant and inspiring librarian Helene Blowers at the Public Library of Charlotte & Mecklenburg County initiated an innovative new staff training program that she called "Learning 2.0—23 Things" (available at http://plcmcl2-things.blogspot.com). 23 Things was an online course, based primarily on a blog platform, that taught staff about Web 2.0 tools such as podcasts, RSS, and wikis. The course was 23 weeks long, with one new lesson each week. Students would access the new week's blog post online, read about and use the new technology, and then post about it on their own individual blogs. These blogs were entered into a tracking log by the students and then reviewed by Blowers as the training coordinator. The class idea was loosely based on the 43Things Web site, which lets individuals track 43 personal goals over time (available at www.43things.com). Numerous libraries have taken advantage of the 23 Things model and folded in additional technologies, techniques, and topics. You can see a list of library-based 23 Things programs through Helene Blowers' list on Delicious (available at http://delicious.com/hblowers/learning 2.0Libraries).

The whole idea is to use the very technologies to teach the class that you are teaching the students about. You learn about blogging by reading, commenting, creating, and posting on blogs. What better way to learn? 23 Things–style courses for library customers can be equally successful if marketed well, involve technologies the library's community wants to learn, and effectively engages those learners immediately.

Topics for the 23 Things Approach

As long as the course topic does not require one-on-one tutoring style hands-on experience with the technology, almost any learning topic will work well with a 23 Things course approach. Institutions have successfully utilized the 23 Things model to teach both basic and advanced technologies, hardware and software, policy, and Web sites. The most important element of any 23 Things course is that the overall course have a unifying theme. These sample themes work well in a 23 Things learning model:

- ▶ Web 2.0 technologies (and now, even the nebulous Web 3.0!)
- ▶ Technology troubleshooting
- ▶ Making the most of your desktop computer
- ▶ Microsoft Office tips and tricks
- ▶ Library's electronic resources and collections

Scope of a 23 Things Program

With a 23 Things model, the scope of the course will depend on the goals of the course. As evidenced by the range of potential topics listed earlier, this class can be complicated or simple, long or short. Even the "23 Things" limitation is an arbitrary one. Many courses reproduced in this model have offered a greater or fewer number of class elements, sometimes 8 and even 40. The timeline for the class should determine, in part, the number of elements, as should the learning goals. Let's say, for example, that the goals of the class are to teach staff how to effectively use Microsoft Office. Deciding on which Office software to cover (e.g., only Word and Excel, or PowerPoint and Outlook too?) will determine how many things you have to teach. The follow-up question is what you want to teach about each piece of software and into how many logical chunks you can break that content. My recommendations are to keep the chunks short enough for digestion within a half hour to an hour and to offer enough information to provide substantial outcomes for the 23 Things course but not too much information that the staff are overwhelmed and simply tune out half of each week's content or ignore the last third of the entire class.

Technology Setup

Because the format of the class is on the Web, the 23 Things model works best if the instructor fully utilizes all of the Web technologies at hand to create a dynamic class. Some examples include asking the students to maintain their own blogs as in the original 23 Things course, adding links to each post to online resources for more information and additional explanation, asking users to comment on others' posts as part of the class, using RSS blending tools to create a master Web page displaying entries from all of the different student blogs, and using audio and video to teach parts of the class.

Staff Participation and Interest

Many believe that one of the reasons that the 23 Things model was so successful was the incentives for staff. The original program gave out MP3 players to each participant and raffled off a laptop and a PDA. Other programs have given staff gift certificates to Amazon or iTunes, buttons, T-shirts, USB drives, toys, professional subscriptions to online services like Flickr or LibraryThing, catered lunches, hours or days of vacation time, and preferred parking spots. The incentives themselves are probably the most effective method for encouraging staff participation. Even if the incentives are relatively inexpensive, staff will be infinitely more likely to participate than if there were no incentives other than the reward of learning itself. So, choose the incentives carefully and advertise the heck out of them when launching your program.

In addition, the name "23 Things" or even "Learning 2.0" may be enough of a buzzword to encourage interest. Because the idea is now some years old, however, for some staff the name has lost its cachet. Now that many libraries and other institutions have already used this model, it may no longer feel as novel to staff, so to instantly rouse interest in the program you can call your class something else. Call it what it's teaching (Microsoft Outlook in 15 Weeks) or be cute (Walking in the Tech Wonderland). The name, subject matter, plus the incentives should be enough to grab most staff interest. As the course is presented with a blog, wiki, or other online technology, the training organizer(s) can also use an intranet RSS feed as an ongoing way to market and remind users of the class. You can use free services like FeedBurner (available at http://feedburner.google.com) to effortlessly turn the RSS feed into an e-mail update for those users who do not use or prefer RSS updates. Finally, follow good general training marketing practices (addressed in Chapter 4).

Examples of Other 23 Things Courses

The number of library 23 Things courses is ever-growing and is currently over 300 (Blowers, http://delicious.com/hblowers/learning2.0Libraries). Here are a few of my favorites:

- ▶ **23 Things on a Stick**: http://23thingsonastick.blogspot.com (Minnesota Multicounty Multitype Library Systems, 2007) and More Things on a Stick: http://morethingsonastick.pbworks.com (Minnesota Multicounty Multitype Library Systems, 2009)

- ▶ **26.2 Things in Boston**: http://boston26dot2.blogspot.com (Jennifer Koerber, 2008)

▶ **Baker's Dozen**: Learning 2.0 Arizona: http://bakersdozen arizona.wetpaint.com (Arizona State Library, Archives, and Public Records and Pima County Public Library, 2008)

▶ **CityLibrariesLearning—discover*play*connect**: http://city librarieslearning.wordpress.com (Townsville CityLibraries, Queensland, Australia, 2009)

▶ **Learning 2.0—23 Things**: http://plcmcl2-things.blogspot.com (Helene Blowers, 2006) and Learning 2.1—Explore . . . Discover . . . Play!: http://explorediscoverplay.ning.com (Public Library of Charlotte & Mecklenburg County, 2009)

▶ **School Library Learning 2.0**: http://schoollibrarylearning2 .blogspot.com/2007/02/23-things_27.html (California School Library Association, 2007)

Online self-paced training has become increasingly popular in the past few years. This type of training is simply more resource efficient for both the instructor and the student, as well as self-paced and repeatable and therefore useful for the student. Have fun with the 23 Things model and think up as many ways to use it as you can and then share those with your colleagues in other libraries, through whatever means, by letting them know what you are doing. Together I believe we can extend this model to even more topics and people.

▶ DEVELOP A TECHNOLOGY PETTING ZOO

Technology petting zoos do not involve iguanas with iPods or sheep with smartphones (although that would be pretty cool, too). Technology petting zoos typically involve a laboratory-style setting with multiple technologies for staff to experiment with, play with, and learn. This approach is most useful for libraries with staff who have until now lacked the opportunity or motivation for hands-on experience with certain technologies, including technologies that library staff should be using on the job and also technologies that library users are employing in their use of library resources and services. The approach can also be wildly successful with library customers, giving people the chance to experience heretofore "mysterious" technology topics like Facebook or iPhone. When provided to groups of people other than library employees, however, security for the devices becomes an added concern. Be prepared to pay for staff to watch each station and device, and have someone available to operate a coat check so that participants can leave their bags and jackets at the door.

Most petting zoos are a one-time event, sometimes held at an "all staff day" in order to expose many people to the technologies in one go. Different technologies are set up in a rotation at individual stations, either spread out around a single room or in multiple rooms if possible. The stations are staffed by "experts," and staff are divided up into groups to rotate around the different stations. Each group should have a small enough number of participants to allow for personalized exposure and time to work with the technology. A good goal is four to six people per group. If there are simply too many staff per group for one rotation (e.g., 50 staff members in 10 groups of 5, at 10 stations, moving in circle to hit all stations), you can instead choose to stagger starting times for the program and move sequentially. For example, Group 1 starts at Station 1 at 10 a.m. and moves through 10 stations, with 20 minutes at each. Group 2 starts at Station 1 at 10:20 a.m., Group 3 starts at 10:40 a.m., and so on.

The event can be as short or as long as is necessary to allow adequate exposure to the various technologies. In order to give context and closure to the learning experience, it's a good idea to begin the day with a lecture-style introduction and end with a debriefing/time for questions. You will also want to provide help manuals, resource guides, cheat sheets, and recommended books/ articles at the stations. These materials should also be linked to from the staff intranet for people to access later. It is also a good idea to photograph, blog, or microblog the event to raise interest in the technology petting zoo's technologies.

See the Hartford County (Maryland) Public Library's blog for their Technology Petting Zoo event as a good example: http://hcpltechfair .blogspot.com. *Library Journal* also has a short video of Infopeople's Cheryl Gould giving a tour of their Technology Petting Zoo for the Association for Rural and Small Libraries: www.libraryjournal.com/flashVideo/element_id/2140272868/taxid/33552.html.

Technologies to Pet

Deciding which technologies to include in your petting zoo is not a perfect process. Much will depend on what technologies your staff must learn immediately for customer service purposes, what technologies the library has access to, and the petting zoo room's network and power capacities. It is a good idea to survey the staff ahead of time to find out which technologies they would like training for and focus on those that would work best in a petting zoo setting (i.e., technologies that can't easily be covered in a computer lab). Here are some effective technology petting zoo station ideas:

▶ **e-Book and e-audiobook station**: Offer a computer with the library's e-book collections' software, a few sample books already downloaded, as well as a collection of portable devices (MP3 player, e-book reader, PDA, etc., and any connection cables) to which to transfer the book.

▶ **RSS and feed readers**: Set up a computer with a few different Web-based and desktop feed readers, and feature several RSS search engines to demonstrate how this works. You can even extend it to feed-building and feed-blending services to demonstrate how to utilize feed content on the library's Web site. You can also include examples of useful feeds from the library world or library Web sites with a good collection of feeds.

▶ **Photographs**: Feature a digital camera, a computer with image-editing software, and a photo-sharing site like Flickr. Also try featuring examples of good library photo-sharing sites. A side benefit is that, by asking participants to use this station's technology, you can obtain photos of the session to promote the training to the rest of the staff.

▶ **Audio**: Offer a digital audio recorder, a computer with audio-editing software, and a blog on which to post the test audio files. Instant podcasting.

▶ **Video**: Offer a digital video recorder, a computer with video-editing software, and a blog on which to post the test video files. Instant videocasting.

▶ **Chat (text, audio, and video)**: Feature a computer with a few different individual chat software options loaded (e.g., AOL's Instant Messaging, Google Talk), a chat aggregator like

Trillian or Meebo, and some audio and video chat through software like Skype or SightSpeed or even through some of the options that automatically feature audio and video.

▶ **Gaming**: One or more stations can feature different gaming consoles, especially those that the library supports through programming or game lending. This can include the Wii, Xbox, PC games, Nintendo DS, PlayStation Portable, or any other console.

▶ **Social networking**: Offer a computer with access to several different social networking sites, both the public and administrative views. Feature the sites on which the library has profiles and/or those that library users use most, like Facebook, MySpace, LinkedIn, and Ning. Also try featuring examples of successful library social networking sites.

▶ **Open source software**: Set up demonstrations of open source software of use in the library: Open Office, Ubuntu, Google Docs, Koha, SOPAC, and anything else of interest to your library staff. See the oss4lib Web site (www.oss4lib.org) for more information on open source software in libraries.

▶ **Online marketing**: Set up a computer with access to social review sites like Yelp, free WiFi directories, community event calendars, iGoogle, and Wikipedia—all sites on which the library should have a presence and hopefully interactions with the public through comments.

▶ **Blogs, microblogs, and wikis**: Set up a computer with access to public and administrative views of a blog (Blogger, WordPress), a microblogging service (Twitter), and a wiki (PBworks), so that content can be added or edited. Also try featuring examples of library and librarian blogs, microblogs, and wikis.

Getting a hold of technologies for the petting zoo is a multi-pronged process. As you can see, the numbers of computers and Internet connections needed quickly add up. First, try to see which technologies can be acquired through library IT, either those that are already on hand or those that they would be willing to purchase for the petting zoo that can also be used for other purposes afterward. Second, try asking which technologies staff have and are willing to lend out for the technology petting zoo. Third, try partnering with big-box stores in your area, retailers who might be able to loan out some flat-screen televisions, MP3 players, gaming systems, projection systems, or other devices to help the day to be successful. Many stores will be more than happy to do so in exchange for signage attributing the donations to their company, and some will even send a technician with the equipment to help operate it (and potentially try to make sales, so watch out for that). Local policies may prohibit such a partnership, but it's definitely worth looking into.

Petting Zoo Setting

The petting zoo setup will depend largely on the number of different technologies you propose to demonstrate and on the number of participants in the session. In either case, you can never have too much space. I recommend having a lecture-style room set up for the opening introduction to the day's activities and for the debriefing as well. This room can be used in the petting zoo rotation as a place for people to rest, eat, drink, and socialize in between sessions. A large meeting room (or multiple rooms) can be used for the petting zoo stations themselves. When setting up the various stations, consider these variables:

▶ Allow enough space around each station for each group's full number of participants.

▶ Think about the volume or physical activity's impact on the space. For example, gaming can be quite loud, and, if setting up Dance Dance Revolution or Wii Tennis, additional space will be required for the physical motions.

▶ Allow buffer space between each station as well so that participants aren't distracted or disturbed by another station's activities.

▶ Offer seating at each station, as well as room to stand, to give participants choices for comfort.

▶ Ensure that there is a good physical flow in the room between the different stations. This can be done by setting up a floor plan and doing a walk-through ahead of time.

▶ Ensure that Internet connections (wired or wireless) are available where they are needed.

▶ Finally, ensure that there are large, clear signs labeling each station as well as signage directing people from one station to the next and to restrooms and exits.

Staff Support

Each station should have a coordinator and, if possible, additional support staff to conduct a demo and then be available to answer questions as the participants experiment. To find effective staff support for the stations, use staff members who have used the technologies on their own already or who are known as the resident experts in the library. Library trainers are a good resource, in addition, as the ability to train is just as important as expertise with the equipment.

If the technology petting zoo will have a large number of participants, it might also be worth it to utilize a few people as hosts to help move people between stations. These staff can also function as "floaters"—floating between different stations and positions to fill in if the station staff needs a break or an extra hand.

Finally, ensuring the support of the library's IT personnel is essential for the success of a technology petting zoo. Not only will they likely be providing much of the equipment, software, and connections, but they will also be instrumental in providing support on the day of the petting zoo—fixing problems as they come up.

The Mobile Zoo

Some institutions have decided to create a mobile technology petting zoo, a lab-in-a-box, if you will. The benefits to this approach are that more people in more locations over a long period of time get to experience the technologies. The disadvantages include the need to maintain and deliver the box and its equipment, the inability to offer large technologies that are not portable (such as large screens and Dance Dance Revolution mats), the lack of as many experts involved to teach the different technologies, the need to purchase and not simply borrow the technologies, and the possibility of loss or theft.

If the library has enough funding or equipment donations to create an effective mobile zoo, a few additional considerations will be necessary to make the setup work well. Decisions about how the staff will use the mobile zoo will need to be made. For example, will there be training materials to accompany the technologies and/or will there be an expert trainer on-site to demonstrate and support the technologies? Also, the library needs to decide how the technologies will be maintained and sent out. Will library IT staff deliver the mobile zoo box? When it's returned, will the technology be checked out to ensure everything is still present and functioning?

In a large, multilocation library system, a mobile lab approach may simply be more practical in order to reach all staff. If it seems that this will work better for your library, be sure to consider all of the issues with loaning equipment, as well as with training, before embarking on the mobile zoo approach.

Equipment Tips and Ideas

Any trainer or IT professional will tell you that if there is a chance that equipment will fail, it will fail. Do a dry run to check all equipment the night before the technology petting zoo (or morning of, if you have time). Check everything: computers, keyboards, mice, projectors, Internet connections, hubs, routers, extension cords, projection surfaces, connection cables, software, and any portable devices like e-book readers and MP3 players. If equipment is being loaned out to the library for the day, label everything (including cables) to ensure that it is returned to its rightful owner. It might also be a good idea to bring a few extra supplies and accessories, such as keyboards, mice, and projector bulbs. It is also necessary to do a dry run of the Internet connections to ensure that they can sustain the simultaneous load impact that will occur during the day of the petting zoo.

▶ UTILIZE ONLINE TRAINING SOURCES

Online training of all kinds has become increasingly popular because of tightening budget issues. Whereas before, online training opportunities were convenient and easy to obtain, now for many institutions they are mandatory or even the only option. As a result, learning how to effectively utilize online training opportunities that already exist out there on the Web somewhere has become vital to expanding and even maintaining our libraries' training offerings to our staff members.

Find Online Training

I have four tips for finding online training resources for use in libraries:

1. My first tip for finding online training materials, classes, or events is to simply conduct a Web search. There is so much out there on the open Web on company or nonprofit Web sites, individual blogs, discussion boards, groups, and on and on. More often than not someone else has done the work for you and can save you a lot of time. The more specific you are with your search terms, the better off you'll be with the results. Also, if you prefer training in a particular format, it's easy to use advanced search techniques to narrow down to a particular file type or to search for videos or Webcasts specifically.

2. Take a look at the official Web sites for the hardware, software, and Web services on which you are training. Database vendors, for example, have a mountain of training resources online, as do office software providers, printer companies, e-mail providers, etc.

3. Put out a call to other professionals using online tools. Try library listservs like PUBLIB (http://lists.webjunction.org/publib) and Web4Lib (http://lists.webjunction.org/web4lib), Lori Reed's Library Learning Google Group (http://groups .google.com/group/librarylearning?hl=en), and social networking sites like LinkedIn or Facebook and their internal library-related groups.

4. Use one of the many subject-specific technology training resource Web sites listed in the Recommended Resources at the end of this book. There are so many great resources on the Web today, but I chose just a few of my favorites to highlight in that section.

Remember—we are library folk! Finding information is what we do. Locating online training resources should be approached the way one would approach a reference interview. Get all the information you can on the specific training needs of your library, and then search away. And any time you find some useful technology training resources, stop for a moment to consider if they would be useful for the library's customer base as well. Add the site to the tech resources list on the library's Web site or as a recommended resource in a blog post, or Tweet it to your library followers. So often, what helps the library staff will also help the library customer.

Incorporate Live Online Training

Live online training is an efficient and effective way to deliver training to a large number of people simultaneously. Furthermore, learners are not required to travel to a training location, learners are able to ask questions of the trainer, and the materials are generally available for access after the class for refreshers or by those unable to attend the live event. Unfortunately, many managers are unfamiliar with the usefulness of online training in the library. The result is that staff are often given time away from floor duties to attend in-person classes but are not given time for online learning, either live or self-paced.

Convincing management that online learning counts is the first step. The second step is emphasizing the importance of online learning in the workplace by marketing various opportunities and making it clear when staff are participating in a class. I suggest tacking an "I AM IN TRAINING—DO NOT DISTURB" sign to the individual's door or even on the back of his or her chair. This both alerts staff to not interrupt the individual and posts a visual reminder that online training is taking place and therefore is important to the institution.

All live online learning is not the same. Webcasts feature live video and audio; Webinars feature live audio only with live slide sharing; and teleconferences feature live audio only. Depending on the individual's learning style and on the material being taught, some techniques will be more effective than others.

Most live online learning in libraries is provided by external agencies. Organizations like WebJunction and Infopeople provide frequent live online training for library staff on a wide range of topics. Electronic resource vendors for library e-books, databases, and online reference services also frequently provide live training opportunities online. Each organization provides e-mail and/or RSS updates on these opportunities so it is easy to stay up-to-date on what's available. A fabulous resource of e-learning resources and sources is "E-learning: Annotated Bibliography for Library Training Programs" (Signorelli, 2009).

If your library decides to provide its own live online learning, there are a number of factors to consider when setting up such a training system:

▶ **Delivery platform**: Decide on the learning platform to be used. Libraries can utilize completely free services such as Skype, SightSpeed, or TokBox to participate in audio or video along with live chat. You can also choose to implement services such as Yugma, GoTo Meeting, or WebEx to share documents, share screens, and provide audio and/or video conferencing. Most services of this type offer free versions for a limited number of simultaneous participants and discounted prices on the paid version of the service for nonprofit institutions like libraries. Figure 3.2 shows an example of how Yugma was used to bring in Char Booth remotely as the fourth panelist at the 2007 Future of Libraries Conference in San Francisco. Pictured from left to right at the table are Sarah Houghton-Jan, Debbie Faires, and Jeremy Kemp; Char Booth is pictured at the top of the screenshot.

▶ **Software**: Some Web conferencing services require specific software or settings on the learners' computers. Get a list of these requirements ahead of time and either alert learners to check their computers before the class or ask IT to make global changes to staff computers.

▶ **Hardware**: If Web conferencing, what equipment does the instructor need? A microphone? A Webcam? Do the learners need any additional equipment?

▶ **Archiving**: It's best to archive any live event on the Web for access afterward. You will likely need to decide if you wish to archive the class on the library's Web site, the service's hosted Web site, or elsewhere. Remember: access is the first priority.

Putting something behind multiple passwords and on an internal network protects it from the public but may disallow staff to access from home or new staff to access without required special log-ins.

No matter who is providing live online learning to your library staff, be sure to give staff time to complete the training. Also provide ample access to the materials and training calendars on the library's intranet.

▶ Figure 3.2: Yugma Conferencing Service

Encourage Self-Paced Online Training

Self-paced online training, sometimes called "unscheduled online training," is the unsung hero of the training world. Self-paced online training can take many forms. These methods have a high impact:

▶ Working through various forms of online tutorials

▶ Listening to podcasts

- ▶ Viewing recorded and archived Webcasts
- ▶ Reading articles, blog posts, discussion boards, and listserv posts
- ▶ Reading e-books or listening to e-audiobooks
- ▶ Viewing videocasts or screencasts
- ▶ Completing asynchronous online courses
- ▶ Browsing the Web sites of libraries and other institutions for ideas

The same managerial acceptance problems that occur with live online training are amplified with self-paced online training. This is because there is nothing "on the calendar," as it were, so it tends to get low priority from both the manager and the learner. So much can be learned online by browsing through the wealth of information available at your own pace and on your own schedule. This is especially true of technology-related information. The newest information is online and probably hasn't made its way into a formal presentation or class yet. Unscheduled learning is certainly a foreign concept to some, but the basic concept is that it consists of learning on your own schedule and at your own pace. Everything else (format, structure, technology) is up for grabs.

In 2006, Stephen Abram posted encouragement on his blog, *Stephen's Lighthouse,* for library staff to take 15 minutes a day to learn something new. He emphasized learning online and focusing on new technologies and Web services. By stressing the importance for everyone to learn, Abram (2006) argued:

> The capacity of the library system for innovation and change is exponentially increased. It also sends a positive message from the library leadership team about the value they place on staff, interaction, learning and relating to their communities and learning. Think for a moment about what 15 minutes a day, or even 15 minutes a week, would do for each of your staff members. Now, multiply that by the total number of staff you have— how much learning is this!?! How much do you believe that much learning can affect the service your users receive?

This idea of 15-minute chunks of learning has been rapidly, and extensively, absorbed into library culture. This method of unscheduled learning is much closer to an organic approach—short, self-paced chunks is how our minds best digest new information. Because these short periods of time have a small per-session impact on the library staff workloads, managers tend to initially be more receptive to this approach instead of asking for hours at a time for online staff training.

When encouraging participation in unscheduled online learning, we also need to consider the staff members' own motivation. Whereas scheduled learning, be it online or in person, offers learners a concrete outcome—completion of a course, attendance at a Webcast—self-paced online learning generally offers less of a formal reward. Two steps can help encourage staff participation: (1) creating a formal way for staff to track and/or request time to participate in self-paced online learning activities; and (2) creating rewards for staff for self-paced online learning participation, such as small gifts or raffle entries for a certain number of learning hours. In addition, like all forms of learning, any self-paced online activities should have a positive impact on staff reviews or evaluations. All methods of training serve to empower staff, improve overall knowledge of all staff, and better the customer service in the library.

▶4

MARKETING

▶ Choose a Marketing Vehicle
▶ Reach Your Audience

▶ CHOOSE A MARKETING VEHICLE

Promoting staff training can be easy and effective with an organized approach. The first step is to consider your audience. What motivates the library's staff to learn? What subjects are they interested in? What subjects do they need to learn to do their jobs well? Which methods of communication do they respond most positively to? By considering these questions, you can choose the most effective methods for marketing the training. And by following a schedule for promotion and completing various steps, training opportunities will have more participants and generate more excitement.

The best advice I can give to any library about marketing training is to send out a weekly staff training newsletter or include a training section in any other regular staff publication. Creating the newsletter using a blog, and offering subscription options via e-mail and RSS, will reach as many staff as possible. You may also find it necessary to send out a blast e-mail to all staff via e-mail with a link to the blog post each week. Make sure that the training section of the intranet also links to this weekly publication.

Talking about training opportunities in as many venues as possible is also highly useful. People usually listen better than they read, and they then have the opportunity to discuss or ask questions about the training, too. Ask individuals to talk about the current training offerings at various committee and team meetings, unit or branch staff meetings, and other library staff events.

Printed material can also help to advertise training opportunities. Printing out a copy of the weekly training newsletter and posting it in staff break rooms, or circulating it among the staff, is a low-investment approach that still raises the visibility of the training. Important and high-impact training opportunities, such as an on-site class from a consultant or a brown bag series, will benefit from an additional push through printed flyers describing the training. These flyers should be colorful and eye-catching, with the training topic or title in huge font, the location and time of the training underneath, and very little other text on the flyer. As with flyers for the public, keep it simple.

For a little extra buzz, use an image generator to create fun training advertisements for use on the library's intranet, weekly newsletter, or printed flyers. Use your creativity and make something fun! My favorites are Add Letter's newspaper headline generator (www.addletters.com/newspaper-generator.htm) and Says-It .com's concert ticket generator (www.says-it.com/concertticket; see Figure 4.1).

The choices are nearly limitless. Additional image generator options are offered by The Generator Blog (http://generatorblog .blogspot.com), ImageGenerator.org (www.imagegenerator.org), and ImageChef (www.imagechef.com). Or do a basic Web search for the type of image generator you are looking for, such as "Las Vegas sign generator." You can also use images to promote training by taking photographs at the training sessions and posting them to

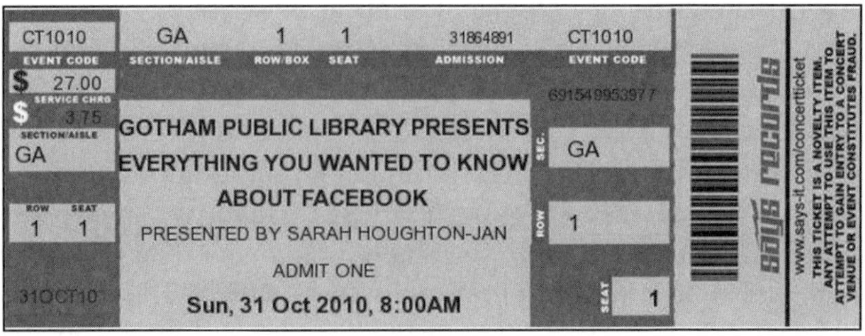

▶ Figure 4.1: Super Simple Ticket Created with the Concert Ticket Generator

the library's Flickr account (especially if you have a Flickr account for staff-related photographs).

▶ REACH YOUR AUDIENCE

When thinking about how to market any training opportunity, regardless of the vehicle, choose your words carefully. Marketers traditionally choose one of six emotional drivers to motivate the audience. You too can benefit by targeting some basic human instincts to get your staff trained. Take a look at these examples and think about what would work best for various topics and different audiences within your library:

- **Guilt**: People know what they should do, so tell them: "Stop putting it off—get trained on our new magazine database."
- **Fear**: Appeal to people's real worries and fears: "Feeling behind on tech? Try our class on Web 2.0 basics."
- **Need for approval**: Target people's sense of getting praised: "Take our class to get noticed by your supervisor."
- **Greed**: Offer people something of value: "Come to the gaming training and enter to win a PlayStation Portable."
- **Ego**: Appeal to a desire for superiority over others: "Complete this three-class series and get the latest certificate in education."
- **Increased knowledge**: Gain knowledge that will help make the job easier: "Attend our MS Excel class to learn to create easy, excellent spreadsheets."

In addition, there are some basic tips when writing any promotional materials. Use color, punctuation, large fonts, alliteration, fun and exciting words, and short snippets of information.

As with all marketing, the earlier you start the better, and the more avenues through which the staff are exposed to the training, the more likely it is that participation will be high. Finally, be sure to send out two reminders to staff before any scheduled class, one a week before and one the day before. Without reminders, more participants are likely to forget or simply reassess the training as a low priority and choose not to attend.

Marketing for training also extends after the event. Send out thank-you e-mails, with links to other upcoming training opportunities, following every class. Also ask participants for evaluations of each training, online resource, and trainer. By asking for participants' opinions, it shows not only that the library cares what they think but also allows the organization to improve offerings in the future. Additionally, offer a Web page with class resources as a follow-up to a training session. This will help reinforce the class material and also offer an avenue to advertise related training opportunities and online resources.

Finally, you can also utilize games as a way to follow up on information presented in a training session. A good example is creating a crossword with clues from terms and concepts presented during the training. The lovely Custom Crossword Generator can make this a whole lot easier (http://pdos.csail.mit.edu/cgi-bin/theme -cword). If you prefer word searches or other games, free generators exist for nearly everything nowadays.

▶5

BEST PRACTICES

> ▶ Address Different Learning Styles
> ▶ Deal with Difficult Learners
> ▶ Schedule a Training Class
> ▶ Create a Learning Environment

Every trainer has his or her own unique way of teaching, but some tried and true best practices exist for nearly everyone. By keeping these methods and tactics in mind when conducting technology training classes for either staff or library patrons, even novice technology trainers can seem like practiced professionals.

▶ ADDRESS DIFFERENT LEARNING STYLES

One of the toughest challenges for a trainer is to find a way to meet the needs of each learner. Because people learn best in different ways, many trainers struggle to find a way to teach the topic at hand in a universally effective manner. The simple answer to this complex challenge is to mix and match different learning methods within the same training. This way, each learner will find something to meet his or her individual needs.

The three major learning styles are visual (pictures, mental images), auditory (verbal instructions, talking it out), and kinesthetic (handling, doing). The way that each of us learns best likely depends on the subject matter. In creating lesson plans and materials for different trainings, consider the topic as well as the most effective way to address all three learning styles. As an example, let's consider a class meant to teach how to post an entry to the library's book recommendation blog. An instructor can meet the needs of various learners by teaching the class in a computer lab setting, demonstrating and verbally describing discrete functions and features (verbal and auditory), and then asking learners to complete exercises completing different tasks (kinesthetic). Stopping to think about how best to meet all of the needs, and then creating materials to best meet these needs with training, will help to make the training as effective as possible by helping as many students as possible to retain the information.

Another aspect that affects people's learning styles is time. While some learners will function effectively in a classroom environment, absorbing information quickly and asking questions, other learners require time to absorb the material and need a chance to follow up with both the material and the instructor. Some of the strategies discussed in Chapter 2 on technology training, including materials and classes, can help with providing enough context for learners of all types. Set up a Web page dedicated to the class materials with the opportunity for learners to comment and ask questions. Send out follow-up e-mails to participants with additional exercises or questions. Hold a formal follow-up session to the class. Make the instructor available after the class for follow-up questions. No training session should result in "intellectual bulimia." We've all had trainings or classes where we thought we were absorbing the material at the time, and maybe even remembered it for a test or quiz, but then everything was purged from our minds as soon as it was convenient. We want our library technology training sessions to result instead in "intellectual absorption." Everything taught should be melded into our consciousness in the right place and easily accessible the next time we need it.

Overall, remember that people will learn most effectively if they care about what they are learning. Demonstrate to every learner an aspect of the training that will make life easier, help him or her to be better at the job, or offer fulfillment of one of the six emotional motivators mentioned in Chapter 4 (guilt, fear, need for approval, greed, ego, or increased knowledge). Training is successful when the instructor engages learners as much as possible, offers them frequent chances to participate and ask questions, and provides as much time to experiment hands-on as possible. Benjamin Franklin said it well: "Tell me and I forget. Teach me and I remember. Involve me and I learn."

▶ DEAL WITH DIFFICULT LEARNERS

If you have ever taught or presented to a group, you have likely experienced the terror of having a reluctant learner or a difficult participant. There are a few categories of difficult learners and strategies for dealing with each. Of course, none of these strategies is foolproof, and every situation is unique. However, you are likely to find success with some of these strategies—certainly more so than if you didn't try anything at all!

▶ **Railroaders:** Some learners can't help but take discussions off in random directions, digressing, and getting away from the point of the training. Persist in gently steering them back on topic, keeping the group on task, and, if necessary, speak with them privately and request that they stay on task. Try statements like "I'd love to talk to you about that during the break" or "It would be fabulous if we had time to talk about all of these topics, but we have only an hour."

▶ **Le Resistance:** There are usually some staff members who will resist particular training topics. This group can be dealt with by privately asking why they are resisting the topic and trying to find a way to motivate them. Often, people simply don't see the connection between what is being taught and how it will help make life better or easier. Make this connection for them. If you discover someone who is consistently resistant, it may be most effective to approach that individual's manager and discuss a coordinated approach to solving the situation.

▶ **Fraidy Cats:** Some people are afraid to play with technology, generally out of a fear that they will break something or that they will look stupid. Fraidy Cats can also take the form of students who do not participate or speak. In order to help these learners, ask them pointed questions during the class about their own experiences (not knowledge), and if they respond with abbreviated answers, ask "Can you say a little bit more about that?" Reassure students at the beginning of the class that we are all here to learn, we're all beginners, and that the technology can't be broken so they should experiment away. If you notice an individual appearing hesitant, talk through the concerns and focus on the learning outcome.

▶ **Egomaniacs**: Somewhat like the Railroaders, Egomaniacs take the class off topic. The difference is that the Egomaniacs focus on their narrow, specific needs and want the entire class to focus on this small subsection of the training topic. Once again, offer to discuss the issue during a break or after the class, but repeatedly redirect the discussion to keep the class on task.

▶ **Self-Appointed Know-It-Alls**: Ahh, yes. These are any trainer's favorite group. These folks take arrogance to a new level by coming in to classes believing they know more than the instructor and taking every opportunity to demonstrate this. Sometimes those in this group even openly show resentment at being taught. This tends to be particularly true of high-level managers, who sometimes take exception to a "lower" staff member being in a position to teach them. If you find someone constantly correcting you, contradicting you, or even taking over the class, acknowledge his or her contributions but assert yourself. You are the instructor for a reason, after all.

Fortunately, most library employees are excited and happy for opportunities to learn. But you may find that those few who resist training will be resentful and angry about being in a class. The most important thing to remember is to approach these resistant learners in a positive way. Stay positive, be calm, be sympathetic, and try your best to see the world from his or her point of view. Oddly enough, many times these resistant learners turn into the library's foremost learning champions.

▶ SCHEDULE A TRAINING CLASS

Location and Setting

In-person trainings can be made or broken by the setting. Get to know the different training facilities available to you in the library, in partner facilities, or even in the community. You may find locations in the least likely places. Some of the best trainings I've had have been small group trainings at a café over lunch. Create a list of the various computer labs, meeting rooms, community rooms, and other facilities available to you.

When setting up a new class, consult the list and think of the best setting based on the number of attendees and type of class (hands-on computer, small groups, lecture-style, etc.). The number of seats and types of seats need to be appropriately matched to the class. While you don't want to hold a three-person class in a huge lecture hall, you also don't want to cram 20 people into a room with a capacity for 15. A good tip is to err on the side of a bigger room.

Of course, the room needs to offer the right setup for your class as well. Hands-on computer classes require a computer lab setup. Small groups require tables around which learners can gather. If the class needs to be flexible and offer lecture and small group set-ups, be sure to find a room that can be quickly and easily changed around (e.g., no heavy tables or chairs that are bolted to the floor).

Other factors come into play too in selecting the right facilities:

▶ **Availability and timing**: Can you get the room when you want it, with some time before and after the class for set-up and take-down? Does the time match up with when the most potential learners will be available?

▶ **Comfort factor**: Are the chairs comfortable? Is there enough room between seats and computer stations for learners to spread out their materials?

▶ **Refreshments**: People like to eat and drink, so make sure that the location allows food and beverages.

▶ **Technology and network**: Do the computers have the right software? Can the network handle simultaneous traffic from all students at once?

▶ **Lighting**: Does the room lighting allow learners to see their screens, the wall screen, and/or the handouts? Is there glare from the windows?

▶ **Sound**: Are the room acoustics good? Will the training disturb others in nearby rooms, or will others be loud enough to disturb you?

▶ **Parking and mass transit**: Is there enough parking for staff on-site? Are there bus stops or other transportation options nearby?

▶ **Room access**: Will there be any problem for students getting into the room at the time of the training? Is the building closed, or is the room locked from the inside?

▶ **Central location**: If the library has multiple locations or branches, hold trainings at a geographically central place or rotate the locations of various trainings.

Registration Tips

Some classes will lend themselves to requiring registration ahead of time, while others may function well on a walk-in basis. If the room is quite large and/or you don't expect an overwhelming response to the class, allowing walk-ins is a great way to encourage flexible participation in a class. You may even end up with more walk-in participants than you would if you required registration. However, if registration is necessary because of a limited number of seats or an institutional requirement for sign-ups, the class ends up requiring a bit more planning. Here are some questions to answer before proceeding with registrations:

▶ How should participants register: through an online or paper form, via e-mail, over the phone?

▶ Do procedures vary for internal and external classes or for scheduled and unscheduled learning? Do they need to incorporate any training or travel costs?

▶ Do participants need verbal or written permission from their supervisors?

▶ How will participants receive confirmation that they are in the class?

My favorite method is to handle registration through a simple online form that either generates an e-mail to the instructor or is automatically deposited into a Web database. Commercial products are available that control event registration. Some libraries already use such systems for patron registration for classes and can use the same system at no additional cost for staff class registrations. Try to keep procedures as simple as possible to encourage as much learning as you can. The more signatures required, the harder the process is to follow; and the longer it is, the more likely it is that the learner will give up. No matter what, make sure that the registration process is clear, documented, and accessible to all staff.

▶ CREATE A LEARNING ENVIRONMENT

The single biggest effect that you can have on staff learning in the library is to consider all aspects of training, evaluation, expectations, and rewards with an eye for creating a culture of learning in your library. Technology is ever-changing, and to succeed in a library one must accept change as a part of everyday living and even thrive on change. A key element of contemporary libraries is working well within our constantly changing environment. Most current staff, however, did not know that the job was going to be this way when they were initially hired. As a result, like most of the rest of the world, libraries have a high percentage of staff members who have a hard time with change.

Libraries are the knowledge centers in our communities. To maintain this position, we need to emphasize the ever-changing information world and the resulting ever-changing technologies in our communities and institutions. Ongoing learning must become a priority in the library, at every level and in every location. The entire organization must understand the priority and promise of ongoing learning and training.

To commit to molding your library into an environment of continuous learning takes money and time. Training participation, and information retention, must be folded in to library staff expectations and evaluations. Training of all kinds must be promoted and supported by management. Creating a learning institution helps to recruit highly skilled staff and to increase staff retention rates. Such a nurturing environment also encourages staff to keep learning on their own. If it's important to the library, it becomes important to the staff. A tried and true technique is to identify local heroes among the staff who believe in the power of training and can act as a grassroots group of lobbyists to show others the blissful effects of technology training on the staff at large. Confidence and excitement are infectious. Spread it!

Management needs to present a united front to staff and encourage learning of all kinds to all staff. Managers should ensure that staff have time to attend scheduled training and to participate in unscheduled learning opportunities. In addition, staff should be encouraged to offer training to their coworkers, and therefore they need to be given time to prepare and deliver training to others. While promoting external trainings helps tremendously, nothing replaces the availability of in-house training opportunities that are tailored specifically to the library's individual needs. Learning should be offered and supported in as many ways, in as many places, and by as many people as possible.

To learn more strategies for creating a learning environment in the library, view Lori Reed's archived Webinar on WebJunction, "Cultivating a Culture of Learning" (www.webjunction.org/events/webinars/webinar-archives/-/articles/content/3936430).

▶6

MEASURES OF SUCCESS

▶ Measure Individual Learning Outcomes

▶ Measure Group Learning Outcomes

▶ Perform Training Evaluations

Libraries consistently launch new projects, services, and ideas but rarely assess their impact or success. Because training is a resource-sensitive undertaking, it is essential to determine the technology training strategies that are most successful. Measuring the success of training in any format can be easy if it is approached in a systematic manner. The library will get the best metrics if library staff are assessed before, during, and after the training. Additionally, the success of individual trainings and trainers should be evaluated. Changes should be made at any stage of the training process to maximize the benefits. Before determining what metrics the library will use to measure the success of technology training, management needs to ascertain the goals for the training for individuals, groups, and the library as a whole. This chapter will help to conclude our ADDIE training model with the "Evaluation" step.

▶ MEASURE INDIVIDUAL LEARNING OUTCOMES

Assessment tips were discussed in Chapter 2 and covered three major methods: self-assessment, peer assessment, and formal testing of staff technology skills. If the library desires numeric metrics as an outcome of a training program, staff must be assessed at the beginning of the program to gauge their baseline skill set. Goals should be set for each individual (which can be a uniform set of goals based on the individual's position within the library) as a result of the initial assessment. If the library's technology skills assessment is broken into categories (hardware, operating systems, search skills, etc.), in addition to the general percentage of skills improvement will be the separate skills metrics in each category. In all assessments, asking for a rating of staff self-confidence in their technology skills is an additional useful metric.

While I generally encourage reassessments to take place once employees have had ample opportunity to receive the training they need in all areas, if the training is spread out over many months it may be helpful to insert one or more additional assessments in the middle of the training program. Training coordinators should provide individual employees and managers with feedback during the entire training cycle. Who is attending classes? Who is showing marked improvement? Keep in mind that individual staff technology skill metrics will likely be something to keep private, with access limited to the staff member himself or herself, the supervisor or manager, and the training coordinator. The following table shows an individual's technology skill level (percentage of skills able to successfully complete or explain) and the resulting improvement over the course of one year. This could work for any form of assessment as long as it was measured numerically.

The average percentages, as well as the individual category percentages, can be useful in determining the need for further training as well as targeting areas for improvement for a future evaluation.

Individual Technology Skill Level Improvement

Knowledge Area	January	June	December
Basic operating system	70%	80%	80%
Web browsers	50%	50%	100%
Microsoft Office	85%	87%	95%
File management	33%	66%	100%
Troubleshooting	75%	82%	87%
Average	63%	73%	92%

Both the percentage of knowledge and the overall percentage of improvement are important. This sample learner improved 29 percentage points from the starting point of 63 percent—this is a nearly 50 percent increase in overall skills. Thus, where you start is just as important as where you end up. This information may help encourage staff to be honest in their initial assessments.

Beyond staff skills, there are a few other metrics that may reflect the state of staff technology skills. Keep track of how many staff, and which staff, attend certain trainings. Does the amount of time that individuals are spending in training on certain topics match up with a subsequent improvement in technology skills? Hopefully yes. It is also useful to keep track of customer service satisfaction as a way to measure staff technology skills success. How satisfied are customers before a concerted training effort for the library staff? How satisfied are the customers six months or one year later? In addition, library management can look at how much innovation is taking place with library staff, either anecdotally or numerically, if such things are measured.

▶ MEASURE GROUP LEARNING OUTCOMES

In addition to evaluating individual improvements in technology skills, it is essential to look at unit or branch improvement as a group and the library's overall improvement. Tracking staff skills in discrete skill categories, such as those listed earlier, and examining group trends may reveal weaknesses in certain skill areas, issues with skills or skill improvement at specific branches or units, or even global problems in the library as a whole. A lack of skill improvement overall in one location may be attributed to a lack of training, but if not, it's the training coordinator's job to try to find the cause of a group problem. If on the whole the entire library staff have received training on a particular topic, but their skills have not improved, this likely indicates a problem with the training. Perhaps it is not being presented in the best format, or the trainer needs a bit of improvement.

As with individual measurements, keep track of the number of trainings and amount of time and their correlation with staff skill improvement. Look at the changes in customer service satisfaction librarywide as well. How much has the training program benefited the library so far? What training needs still remain? What organizational or personal changes need to be addressed in order for the library to meet its goals?

▶ PERFORM TRAINING EVALUATIONS

A final metric for evaluating the success of a training program is staff feedback on the trainings and trainers. If employees are going to be required to improve their technology skills, then they need to receive adequate training from good trainers in order to meet the goal. Ensuring that the training being offered is of good quality is a mandatory step in any training program with hopes of success.

After every training session, both sessions provided internally and sessions obtained externally from other organizations, be sure to provide learners with the opportunity to fill out an evaluation form about the training. In addition, ask learners to fill out evaluations of any self-paced online training resources after they finish with the resource (e.g., evaluating a tech training tutorial Web site or a specific journal or article). Training evaluations can be as complex or simple as you desire. A simple evaluation can be a two-part question: *Would you recommend this training to a colleague? Why or why not?* This simple approach works very well for short classes, informal learning opportunities, and even for surveying library customers after library staff have provided a class for them.

If you want more details, and specific metrics, about the efficacy of the training and the trainer, then you can offer a multiquestion evaluation. These are some recommended questions:

- ▶ How would you rate the training overall on a scale of 1–10, with 1 being poor and 10 being excellent?
- ▶ How would you rate the instructor's overall effectiveness on a scale of 1–10?
- ▶ How would you rate the instructor's training style on a scale of 1–10?
- ▶ How would you rate the instructor's knowledge of the topic on a scale of 1–10?

▶ How much did you learn today: more than you expected, less than you expected, what you expected, or as much as you could absorb?

▶ Was the pace of the workshop too fast, too slow, or just right?

▶ Were the supporting handouts and other materials useful (yes or no)?

▶ How would you change the class?

▶ Do you have any additional comments on this training?

▶ Do you have any suggestions for new training topics?

A training evaluation can include any number of these questions or any others applicable to your institution's situation.

Whichever evaluation method you choose, be consistent in offering the same form at all trainings, and making sure that it is indeed offered at all trainings. The results should be reviewed by the training coordinator (if there is one) and a high-level manager. This ensures that at least one person other than the trainer himself or herself is reviewing the effectiveness and can make recommendations regarding changes.

Beginning a technology training program can seem overwhelming at the start. Instead of approaching everything at once, take it step by step. Use the parts of this book that are useful to you, that fit your library's unique situation, and be proud that you are taking steps to enhance the knowledge and customer service in your library. Whether you are prepping a training program for a system of hundreds of employees or a personalized program for everyone in your five-person library, this book will help guide you through the steps you need to take.

Finally, remember to try new things. Push the boundaries of what your library has done in the past. Encourage all staff to step up their skills. With so many libraries operating on past practices of limited staff technology training, or even limited training of any type, it's easy to become complacent and let things continue as they have. Take a chance. Break with the past. Make a difference. Remember—if you never cross the line, you rely on others to tell you where the line is. Find that line, and take a step over it. You'll be happy with what you find on the other side.

RECOMMENDED RESOURCES

The following lists include resources cited in the book as well as additional resources that technology trainers will find helpful in the pursuit of training nirvana.

▶ TECHNOLOGY TERMINOLOGY GLOSSARIES

InfoPlease Computer Glossary. Available: www.infoplease.com/ipa/A0006024.html (accessed December 9, 2009).

TechDictionary.com. Available: http://techdictionary.com (accessed December 9, 2009).

TechWeb TechEncyclopedia. Available: www.techweb.com/encyclopedia (accessed December 9, 2009).

Webopedia. Available: http://webopedia.internet.com (accessed December 9, 2009).

WhatIs.com. Available: http://whatis.techtarget.com (accessed December 9, 2009).

▶ GENERAL TECHNOLOGY TUTORIAL CLEARINGHOUSES

Akron Summit County Public Library (Akron, Ohio) Computer Training Class Handouts. Available: http://ascpl.lib.oh.us/training/handouts.html (accessed December 9, 2009).

Akron Summit County Public Library (Akron, Ohio) Computer Training Tutorials List. Available: http://ascpl.lib.oh.us/training/tutorials.html (accessed December 9, 2009).

Anniston Library (Anniston, Alabama) Computer/Internet Tutorials. Available: www.anniston.lib.al.us/computerInternettutorial .htm (accessed December 9, 2009).

College of the Canyons (Santa Clarita, California) Computer Skills Tutorials. Available: http://psychology230.tripod.com/canyons _online/id4.html (accessed December 9, 2009).

Common Craft "Technology in Plain English" Video Tutorials. Available: www.commoncraft.com/videos (accessed December 9, 2009).

Computer HELP! from Memphis Public Library (Memphis, Tennessee). Available: http://memphiscomputers.blogspot.com (accessed December 9, 2009).

Computer Training Tutorials via Delicious. Available: http://del .icio.us/computertutorials (accessed December 9, 2009).

eHow's Computer Section. Available: www.ehow.com/guide_5 -computers.html (accessed December 9, 2009).

GeekGirl's Plain-English Computing. Available: www.geekgirls.com (accessed December 9, 2009).

HCPL (Harford County Public Library) (Belcamp, Maryland) Tech Fair Blog. Available: http://hcpltechfair.blogspot.com (accessed December 9, 2009).

Help2Go. Available: www.help2go.com (accessed December 9, 2009).

HelpWithPCs.com. Available: www.helpwithpcs.com (accessed December 9, 2009).

Hennepin County Library's (Minnetonka, Minnesota) Staff Extranet (Public & Staff Training Resources). Available: http://hclib .org/extranet (accessed December 9, 2009).

HowStuffWorks Computer Channel. Available: http://computer .howstuffworks.com (accessed December 9, 2009).

Infopeople Archived Webcasts and Webinars. Available: http:// infopeople.org/training/webcasts/list/archived (accessed December 9, 2009).

Infopeople Past Workshop Materials. Available: http://infopeople .org/training/past/index.html (accessed December 9, 2009).

LearnTheNet. Available: www.learnthenet.com/english/index.html (accessed December 9, 2009).

Library Support Staff Free Online Learning Sites List. Available: www.librarysupportstaff.com/ed4you.html (accessed December 9, 2009).

LSLC (Library System of Lancaster County) (Lancaster, Pennsylvania) Training Blog. Available: http://lslctraining.blogspot.com (accessed December 9, 2009).

LYRASIS Classes and Events. Available: www.lyrasis.org/Classes -and-Events.aspx (accessed December 9, 2009).

MalekTips. Available: http://malektips.com (accessed December 9, 2009).

Milwaukee Public Library's (Milwaukee, Wisconsin) Computer Curriculums (English & Spanish). Available: www.mpl.org/file/ computer_curriculums.htm (accessed December 9, 2009).

MPLIC (Memphis Public Library and Information Center) (Memphis, Tennessee) ILS & Tech Train Blog. Available: http:// mplictechtrain.blogspot.com (accessed December 9, 2009).

MRRL (Missouri River Regional Library) (Jefferson City, Missouri) Learning *Library* 2.0—Lessons. Available: http:// mrrl1.blogspot.com/index.html (accessed December 9, 2009).

Results through Training—Activities and Exercises. Available: www .rttworks.com/index/free_resources/activities_%26_exercises (accessed December 9, 2009).

Southern Ontario Library Service (Toronto, Ontario) Clearinghouse of Professional Information. Available: www.sols.org/ links/clearinghouse/index.htm (accessed December 9, 2009).

The Technology Topics Brown Bag Series at University of Colorado (Boulder, Colorado-Boulder) (by Doris Cheung). Available: www.colorado.edu/law/faculty/employeeInfo/techbrown bag_sessions.htm (accessed December 9, 2009).

TechSoup's Learning Center. Available: http://techsoup.org/ learningcenter/index.cfm (accessed December 9, 2009).

TechTutorials.net. Available: www.techtutorials.net (accessed December 9, 2009).

WebJunction Course Catalog. Available: www.webjunction.org/catalog (accessed December 9, 2009).

WebJunction Technology Skills Central. Available: www.webjunction.org/technology (accessed December 9, 2009).

WebJunction Training and Development Section. Available: www.webjunction.org/training (accessed December 9, 2009).

▶ SUBJECT-SPECIFIC TECHNOLOGY TUTORIALS

Basic Computer Skills

Advanced Mousing. Available: http://getit.rutgers.edu/tutorials/mousing/index.html (accessed December 9, 2009).

Basic Computer Skills and File Management from University of Maryland University College (Adelphi, Maryland). Available: www.umuc.edu/facdev/basic_skills/basic_skills.html (accessed December 9, 2009).

Desktop Configuration. Available: http://infopeople.org/ training/past/2007/desktop (accessed December 9, 2009).

Mouserobics from Central Kansas Library System (Great Bend, Kansas). Available: www.ckls.org/~crippel/computerlab/tutorials/mouse/page1.html (accessed December 9, 2009).

Mouse Skills from Highland Park Public Library (Highland Park, Illinois). Available: http://hplibrary.org/programs/Web_mouseclas/mouse_class.htm (accessed December 9, 2009).

Mousing Around from Palm Beach County Library (West Palm Beach, Florida). Available: www.pbclibrary.org/mousing (accessed December 9, 2009).

New User Tutorial. Available: http://tech.tln.lib.mi.us/tutor/welcome.htm (accessed December 9, 2009).

E-mail

E-mail Technical and Etiquette Tutorial. Available: www.Websearchguide.ca/communicate/mailfram.htm (accessed December 9, 2009).

Mastering Basic E-mail Skills. Available: www.ctdlc.org/ remediation/indexe-mail.html (accessed December 9, 2009).

Image Software

Editing Your Digital Images Without the Mystery. Available: http://arstechnica.com/guides/tweaks/mystery.ars (accessed December 9, 2009).

Photoshop Elements for Libraries. Available: http://infopeople .org/training/past/2008/photoElem6 (accessed December 9, 2009).

Microsoft Office

Basic Word Processing Skills. Available: www.ctdlc.org/ remediation/indexWord.html (accessed December 9, 2009).

Increasing Your PowerPoint Skills. Available: http://infopeople .org/training/past/2006/increasing-ppt (accessed December 9, 2009).

Microsoft Office How-To Articles. Available: www.microsoft.com/ education/tutorials.mspx (accessed December 9, 2009).

Microsoft Word Modules. Available: www.Internet4classrooms .com/on-line_word.htm (accessed December 9, 2009).

Searching the Web

Bare Bones 101: A Basic Tutorial on Searching the Web. Available: www.sc.edu/beaufort/library/pages/bones/bones.shtml (accessed December 9, 2009).

Best Search Tools Chart. Available: www.infopeople.org/search/ chart.html (accessed December 9, 2009).

Finding Information on the Web. Available: www.lib.berkeley .edu/TeachingLib/Guides/Internet/FindInfo.html (accessed December 9, 2009).

Google Guide. Available: www.googleguide.com (accessed December 9, 2009).

Internet Searching: Advanced. Available: www.searchengineshow down.com/strat/advancedsearch.shtml (accessed December 9, 2009).

Internet Searching: Basic. Available: www.searchengineshowdown
.com/strat/basicsearch.html (accessed December 9, 2009).

Web 2.0: Searching Innovations. Available: http://infopeople
.org/training/past/2007/web20-searching (accessed December 9, 2009).

Web Search Guide. Available: www.websearchguide.ca/tutorials/
tocfram.htm (accessed December 9, 2009).

Web Topics—Other

Augmenting Teaching and Learning with Social Software. Available: http://atlss.umwblogs.org (accessed December 9, 2009).

Five Weeks to a Social Library. Available: www.sociallibraries.com/
course/node (accessed December 9, 2009).

Flickr Information and Training Resources. Available: www.nlc
.state.ne.us/Netserv/flickr.html (accessed December 9, 2009).

Introduction to Blogging. Available: www.blogbasics.com/blog-tutorial-1-1.php (accessed December 9, 2009).

Practical Podcasting and Videocasting. Available: http://
infopeople.org/training/past/2008/podcasting (accessed December 9, 2009).

Twitter Basics for Non-Techies. Available: www.slideshare.net/
starpath/twitter-basics-presentation (accessed December 9, 2009).

Using Web 2.0 Tools for Staff Training. Available: http://
infopeople.org/training/past/2008/staff-training (accessed December 9, 2009).

Web 2.0: A Hands-On Introduction for Library Staff. Available:
http://infopeople.org/training/past/2007/hands-on (accessed December 9, 2009).

▶ LIBRARY TRAINING BLOGS TO WATCH

Almost Bald Trainer Blog (Maurice Coleman). Available: http://
baldgeek.wordpress.com (accessed December 9, 2009).

BlogJunction (WebJunction staff). Available: http://blog .webjunctionworks.org (accessed December 9, 2009).

Building Creative Bridges (Paul Signorelli). Available: http:// buildingcreativebridges.wordpress.com (accessed December 9, 2009).

Librarian by Day (Bobbi L. Newman). Available: http:// librarianbyday.net (accessed December 9, 2009).

Library Garden (group blog with Peter Bromberg, Janie Hermann, and others). Available: http://librarygarden.net/ (accessed December 9, 2009).

Library Trainer Blog (Lori Reed). Available: http://librarytrainer .com (accessed December 9, 2009).

PAFA.net (Polly Alida Farrington). Available: http://blog.pafa.net (accessed December 9, 2009).

Rapid eLearning Blog (Tom Kuhlmann). Available: www. articulate.com/rapid-elearning (accessed December 9, 2009).

T Is for Training (group podcast run by Maurice Coleman). Available: http://tisfortraining.wordpress.com (accessed December 9, 2009).

Tech from the Non-Techie (Beth Tribe). Available: http:// notatech.wordpress.com (accessed December 9, 2009).

▶ TECHNOLOGY TRAINING BOOKS

Barbazette, Jean. 2001. *The Trainer's Support Handbook: A Guide to Managing the Administrative Details of Training.* New York: McGraw Hill.

Biech, Elaine. 2005. *Training for Dummies.* Indianapolis: Wiley.

Brandt, D. Scott. 2002. *Teaching Technology: A How-To-Do-It Manual for Librarians.* New York: Neal-Schuman.

Clothier, Paul. 1996. *The Complete Computer Trainer.* New York: McGraw Hill.

Gerding, Stephanie. 2007. *The Accidental Technology Trainer: A Guide for Libraries.* Medford, NJ: Information Today.

Houghton, Sarah. 2007. *Technology Competencies and Training. Library Technology Reports* 43: 2. Chicago: ALA TechSource.

Meier, Dave. 2000. *Accelerated Learning Handbook: A Creative Guide to Designing and Delivering Easier, More Effective Training.* New York: McGraw Hill, pp. 9–11.

Miner, Nanette. 2006. *The Accidental Trainer: A Reference Manual for the Small, Part-Time, or One-Person Training Department.* Indianapolis: Pfeiffer & Wiley.

Molberg, Andrea. 2003. *Making Live Training Lively: 50 Tips for Engaging Your Audience, A Crisp Fifty-Minute Book.* Boston: Thomson Course Technology.

Pike, Robert W. 2003. *Creative Training Techniques Handbook: Tips, Tactics, & How Tos for Delivering Effective Training,* 3rd ed. Amherst, MA: Harvard Press.

Stolovitch, Harold. 2009. *Telling Ain't Training.* Alexandria, VA: ASTD Press.

▶ TECHNOLOGY TRAINING ARTICLES, CHAPTERS, AND BLOG POSTS

Abram, Stephen. 2006. *Stephen's Lighthouse: Very Cool Learning 2.0.* August 4. Available: http://stephenslighthouse.sirsi.com/archives/2006/08/very_cool_libra.html (accessed December 9, 2009).

Gerding, Stephanie. 2003. "Training Technology Trainers: Lessons from the River." *Computers in Libraries* 23, no. 8 (September).

Gordon, Rachel Singer and Michael Stephens. 2006. "Ten Tips for Technology Training." *Computers in Libraries* 26, no. 5 (May).

Gray, Carolyn M. 1983. "Technology and the Academic Library Staff or the Resurgence of the Luddites." In *Professional Competencies—Technology and the Librarian,* edited by L.C. Smith. Urbana: Graduate School of Library and Information Science, University of Illinois, Urbana–Champaign, pp. 69–76.

Hough, Brenda. 2006 "Teaching People to Be Savvy Travelers in a Technological World." *Computers in Libraries* (May): 9–12.

Massis, Bruce E. 2001. "How to Create and Implement a Technology Training Program." *American Libraries* 49+.

McGuire, Charlene. 2005. "Technology Core Skills for Kansas Library Workers." Kansas Tech Consultants Blog. July 27. Available: http://kansaslibtech.blogspot.com/2005/07/technology-core-competencies.html (accessed December 9, 2009).

Reeves, Thomas C. 2007. "Do Generational Differences Matter in Instructional Design?" September 12. Instructional Technology Forum. Available: http://it.coe.uga.edu/itforum/Paper104/ReevesITForumJan08.pdf (accessed December 9, 2009).

Schmidt, Aaron. 2005. "Walking Paper: Tech Needs Pyramid." January 3. Available: www.walkingpaper.org/115 (accessed December 9, 2009).

Signorelli, Paul. 2009. "E-learning: Annotated Bibliography for Library Training Programs." Paul Signorelli and Associates. June 4. Available http://paulsignorelli.com/PDFs/Bibliography—E-learning.pdf (accessed December 9, 2009).

Woodsworth, Anne. 1997. "New Library Competencies: Our Roles Must Be Defined within the Context of a Global Digital Information Infrastructure, Not Just a Library with Four Walls." *Library Journal* (May 15): 46.

▶ FEATURED LEARNING 2.0 PROGRAMS AND RESOURCES

26.2 Things in Boston (Boston Regional Library System, Boston, Massachusetts). Available: http://boston26dot2.blogspot.com (accessed December 9, 2009).

43 Things. Available: www.43things.com (accessed December 9, 2009).

Baker's Dozen: Learning 2.0 Arizona (Pima County Library and Arizona State Library, Arizona). Available: http://bakersdozenarizona.wetpaint.com (accessed December 9, 2009).

California School Library Association's 23 Things. Available: http://schoollibrarylearning2.blogspot.com/2007/02/23-things_27.html (accessed December 9, 2009).

hblowers's learning2.0Libraries Bookmarks. Available: http://delicious.com/hblowers/learning2.0Libraries (accessed December 9, 2009).

Minnesota Multicounty Multitype Library Systems' (Minnesota) 23 Things on a Stick. Available: http://23thingsonastick.blogspot.com (accessed December 9, 2009).

Minnesota Multicounty Multitype Library Systems' (Minnesota) More Things on a Stick. Available: http://morethingsonastick.pbworks.com (accessed December 9, 2009).

Public Library of Charlotte & Mecklenburg County's (Charlotte, North Carolina) Explore . . . Discover . . . Play! Available: http://explorediscoverplay.ning.com (accessed December 9, 2009).

Public Library of Charlotte & Mecklenburg County's (Charlotte, North Carolina) Learning 2.0—23 Things. Available: http://plcmcl2-things.blogspot.com (accessed December 9, 2009).

Townsville City Libraries' (Townsville, Queensland, Australia) discover*play*connect. Available: http://citylibrarieslearning.wordpress.com/about (accessed December 9, 2009).

▶ FEATURED WEB TOOLS

Concert Ticket Generator. Available: www.says-it.com/concertticket (accessed December 9, 2009).

Custom Crossword Generator. Available: http://pdos.csail.mit.edu/cgi-bin/theme-cword (accessed December 9, 2009).

Diploma Generator. Available: www.addletters.com/diploma-generator.htm (accessed December 9, 2009).

FeedBurner. Available: http://feedburner.google.com (accessed December 9, 2009).

Flickr. Available: www.flickr.com (accessed December 9, 2009).

The Generator Blog. Available: http://generatorblog.blogspot.com (accessed December 9, 2009).

Google Docs. Available: http://docs.google.com (accessed December 9, 2009).

GoToMeeting. Available: www.gotomeeting.com (accessed December 9, 2009).

ImageChef. Available: www.imagechef.com (accessed December 9, 2009).

ImageGenerator.org. Available: www.imagegenerator.org (accessed December 9, 2009).

Kipp Brothers Toys. Available: www.kipptoys.com/default.aspx (accessed December 9, 2009).

LibraryThing. Available: www.librarything.com (accessed December 9, 2009).

Lolcats 'n' Funny Pictures of Cats. Available: http://icanhascheezburger.com (accessed December 9, 2009).

Newspaper Headline Generator. Available: www.addletters.com/makepic.php?f=newspaper-generator (accessed December 9, 2009).

SightSpeed. Available: www.sightspeed.com (accessed December 9, 2009).

Skype. Available: www.skype.com (accessed December 9, 2009).

Slideshare. Available: www.slideshare.com (accessed December 9, 2009).

SurveyMonkey. Available: www.surveymonkey.com (accessed December 9, 2009).

TechAtlas. Available: www.techatlas.org (accessed December 9, 2009).

TokBox. Available: www.tokbox.com (accessed December 9, 2009).

WebEx. Available: www.webex.com (accessed December 9, 2009).

Yugma. Available: www.yugma.com (accessed December 9, 2009).

Zoomerang. Available: www.zoomerang.com (accessed December 9, 2009).

▶ OTHER WEB RESOURCES FOR TECH TRAINERS

The Accidental Trainer. Available: www.theaccidentaltrainer.com (accessed December 9, 2009).

ALA Learning. Available: http://alalearning.org (accessed December 9, 2009).

American Society for Training and Development. Available: www.astd.org (accessed December 9, 2009).

Competency Index for the Library Field from WebJunction. Available: www.webjunction.org/competencies (accessed December 9, 2009).

Library Learning Google Group. Available: http://groups.google.com/group/librarylearning?lnk=srg (accessed December 9, 2009).

New Jersey's Train-the-Trainer: Creating a Community of Library Instructors. Available: www.sjrlc.org/ttt.htm (accessed December 9, 2009).

oss4lib: Open Source Systems for Libraries. Available: www.oss4lib.org/StaffDevelop.org (accessed December 9, 2009).

Presentation Zen. Available: www.presentationzen.com (accessed December 9, 2009).

Professional Development Articles (collected by Jamie McKenzie). Available: http://staffdevelop.org/articles.html (accessed December 9, 2009).

Summit Collaborative Toolkit. Available: www.summitcollaborative.com/cwpm.html (accessed December 9, 2009).

T Is for Training Google Group. Available: http://groups.google.com/group/tisfortraining?pli=1 (accessed December 9, 2009).

Teaching Tips from the University of Hawaii–Honolulu Community College Faculty (Honolulu, Hawaii). Available: http://honolulu.hawaii.edu/intranet/committees/FacDevCom/guidebk/teachtip/teachtip.htm (accessed December 9, 2009).

Technology Petting Zoo from Infopeople. Available: www.libraryjournal.com/flashVideo/element_id/2140272868/taxid/33552.html (accessed December 9, 2009).

Train the Trainer Library Workshops from Infopeople. Available: http://infopeople.org/training/past/2004/train-trainer-gould/ (accessed December 9, 2009).

Trainers Warehouse. Available: www.trainerswarehouse.com (accessed December 9, 2009).

The Training Doctor. Available: www.trainingdr.com/articles.htm (accessed December 9, 2009).

Traveling Technology Petting Zoo Workshops from Infopeople. Available: http://infopeople.org/training/past/2008/petting (accessed December 9, 2009).

Tutorials 2.0: Teaching the Public and Training Staff with Online Screencasts. Available: http://infopeople.org/training/past/2008/screencasts (accessed December 9, 2009).

WebJunction: Creating a Culture of Learning (Webinar by Lori Reed). Available: www.webjunction.org/events/webinars/webinar-archives/-/articles/content/3936430 (accessed December 9, 2009).

BIBLIOGRAPHY

Abram, Stephen. 2006. "Stephen's Lighthouse: Very Cool Learning 2.0." Available: http://stephenslighthouse.sirsi.com/archives/2006/08/very_cool_libra.html (accessed December 9, 2009).

Add Letters. 2009. Diploma Generator. Available: www.addletters.com/diploma-generator.htm (accessed December 9, 2009).

————. 2009. Newspaper Headline Generator. Available: www.addletters.com/makepic.php?f=newspaper-generator (accessed December 9, 2009).

Arizona State Library, Archives, and Public Records and Pima County Public Library. 2008. "Baker's Dozen: Learning 2.0 Arizona." Available: http://bakersdozenarizona.wetpaint.com (accessed December 9, 2009).

Blowers, Helene. 2006. "Learning 2.0—23 Things." Available: http://plcmcl2-things.blogspot.com (accessed December 9, 2009).

————. 2009. hblowers's learning2.0Libraries Bookmarks. Available: http://delicious.com/hblowers/learning2.0 Libraries (accessed December 9, 2009).

Brandt, D. Scott. 2002. *Teaching Technology: A How-To-Do-It Manual for Librarians.* New York: Neal-Schuman.

California School Library Association. 2007. "The 23 Things." Available: http://schoollibrarylearning2.blogspot.com/2007/02/23-things_27.html (accessed December 9, 2009).

Cheung, Doris. "The Technology Topics Brown Bag Series." Available: www.colorado.edu/law/faculty/employeeInfo/tech brownbag_sessions.htm (accessed December 9, 2009).

FeedBurner. Available: http://feedburner.google.com (accessed December 9, 2009).

Flickr. Available: www.flickr.com (accessed December 9, 2009).

Gerding, Stephanie. 2007. *The Accidental Technology Trainer: A Guide for Libraries.* Medford, NJ: Information Today.

Gordon, Rachel Singer and Michael Stephens. 2006. "Ten Tips for Technology Training." *Computers in Libraries* 26, no. 5 (May): 34–35.

Gray, Carolyn M. 1983. "Technology and the Academic Library Staff or the Resurgence of the Luddites." In *Professional Competencies—Technology and the Librarian,* edited by L.C. Smith. Urbana: Graduate School of Library and Information Science—University of Illinois, Urbana–Champaign, pp. 69–76.

Hartford County Public Library. 2008. HCPL Tech Fair Blog. Available: http://hcpltechfair.blogspot.com (accessed December 9, 2009).

Hough, Brenda. 2006. "Teaching People to Be Savvy Travelers in a Technological World." *Computers in Libraries* May: 9–12.

ImageChef, Inc. 2009. ImageChef. Available: www.imagechef.com (accessed December 9, 2009).

ImageGenerator.org. 2009. Image Generator. Available: www.imagegenerator.org (accessed December 9, 2009).

Infopeople. 2009. "Train the Trainer Library Workshops." Available: http://infopeople.org/training/past/2004/train-trainer-gould/ (accessed December 9, 2009).

Kipp Brothers Online. 2009. "Toys & Novelties." Available: www.kipptoys.com/default.aspx (accessed December 9, 2009).

Koerber, Jennifer. 2008. 26.2 Things in Boston Blog. Available: http://boston26dot2.blogspot.com (accessed December 9, 2009).

Library Journal. 2008. "Infopeople's Technology Petting Zoo." Available: www.libraryjournal.com/flashVideo/element_id/2140272868/taxid/33552.html (accessed December 9, 2009).

Massis, Bruce E. 2001. "How to Create and Implement a Technology Training Program." *American Libraries* 32, no. 9: 49–51.

McGuire, Charlene. 2005. "Technology Core Skills for Kansas Library Workers." Kansas Tech Consultants Blog, July 27. Available: http://kansaslibtech.blogspot.com/2005/07/technology -core-competencies.html (accessed December 9, 2009).

Minnesota Multicounty Multitype Library Systems. 2007. Available: http://23thingsonastick.blogspot.com (accessed December 9, 2009).

———. 2009. Available: http://morethingsonastick.pbworks.com (accessed December 9, 2009).

Morris, Robert. 2009. Custom Crossword Generator. Available: http://pdos.csail.mit.edu/cgi-bin/theme-cword (accessed December 9, 2009).

oss4lib Community. 2009. "oss4lib: Open Source Systems for Libraries." Available: www.oss4lib.org (accessed December 9, 2009).

Pet Holdings, Inc. 2009. "Lolcats 'n' Funny Pictures of Cats." Available: http://icanhascheezburger.com (accessed December 9, 2009).

Presurfer. 2009. The Generator Blog. Available: http:// generatorblog.blogspot.com (accessed December 9, 2009).

Public Library of Charlotte & Mecklenburg County. 2009. Available: http://explorediscoverplay.ning.com (accessed December 9, 2009).

Reed, Lori. 2008. "WebJunction: Cultivating a Culture of Learning." Available: www.webjunction.org/events/webinars/ webinar-archives/-/articles/content/3936430 (accessed December 9, 2009).

———. 2009. LibraryLearning. http://groups.google.com/ group/librarylearning?hl=en (accessed December 9, 2009).

Reeves, Thomas C. 2007. "Do Generational Differences Matter in Instructional Design?" Instructional Technology Forum, September 12. Available: http://it.coe.uga.edu/itforum/ Paper104/ReevesITForumJan08.pdf (accessed December 9, 2009).

Robot Co-op. 2004. "43 Things." www.43things.com (accessed December 9, 2009).

Says-It.com. 2009. Concert Ticket Generator. Available: www.says-it.com/concertticket (accessed December 9, 2009).

Schmidt, A. 2005. "Walking Paper: Tech Needs Pyramid." Available: www.walkingpaper.org/115 (accessed December 9, 2009).

Signorelli, Paul. 2009. "E-learning: Annotated Bibliography for Library Training Programs." Paul Signorelli and Associates. Available: http://paulsignorelli.com/PDFs/Bibliography—E-learning.pdf (accessed December 9, 2009).

Townsville City Libraries. 2009. "CityLibrariesLearning—discover* play*connect." Available: http://citylibrarieslearning.word press.com/about (accessed December 9, 2009).

Woodsworth, Anne. 1997. "New Library Competencies: Our Roles Must Be Defined within the Context of a Global Digital Information Infrastructure, Not Just a Library with Four Walls." *Library Journal* May 15: 46.

INDEX

Page numbers followed by the letter "f" indicate figures.

ABOUT THE AUTHOR

Sarah Houghton-Jan is the Digital Futures Manager for the San José Public Library. Sarah was named a 2009 *Library Journal* Mover & Shaker and is active in California's library training organization, Infopeople. She is a well-traveled consultant, speaker, and technology instructor and has been published widely in both library and technology publications. Sarah is also the author of Librarian in Black, the award-winning blog about library technology issues and resources. She lives in San Rafael, California, with her librarian husband and their definitively non-librarian cat.